Context and Complexity

Magoroh Maruyama
Editor

Context and Complexity

Cultivating Contextual Understanding

With 29 Illustrations

Springer-Verlag
New York Berlin Heidelberg London Paris
Tokyo Hong Kong Barcelona Budapest

Magoroh Maruyama, PhD
School of International Politics,
Economics, and Business
Aoyama Gakuin University
Shibuya, Tokyo 150
Japan

Library of Congress Cataloging-in-Publication Data
Context and complexity: cultivating contextual understanding/
Magoroh Maruyama, editor.
p. cm.
Includes bibliographical references.
ISBN-13:978-1-4612-7660-9
1. Communication in management. I. Maruyama, Magoroh.
HD 30.3.C657 1991
658.4'5—dc20 91-17242
CIP

Printed on acid-free paper.

Softcover reprint of the hardcover 1st edition 1992

Typeset by Best-Set Typesetting Ltd., Quarry Bay, Hong Kong.

9 8 7 6 5 4 3 2 1

ISBN-13:978-1-4612-7660-9 e-ISBN-13:978-1-4612-2768-7
DOI: 10.1007/978-1-4612-2768-7

Contents

Contributors

Marcelo Diamand, Faculty of Engineering, University of Buenos Aires, Buenos Aires 1638, Argentina

Peter Gomez, Professor of Management, University of St. Gallen, 9000 St. Gallen, Switzerland

Enrique G. Herrscher, Faculty of Economic Sciences, University of Buenos Aires, Buenos Aires 1004, Argentina

Roberto M. Herrscher, Faculty of Social Sciences, University of Buenos Aires, Buenos Aires 1004, Argentina

Magoroh Maruyama, School of International Politics, Economics, and Business, Aoyama Gakuin University, Tokyo 150, Japan

Edgar Morin, Centre d'études Transdisciplinaires, École des Hautes Études en Sciences Sociales, 44 rue de la Tour, 75116, Paris

Kenji Okuda, Kaminoge 4–30–8, Setagaya-ku, Tokyo 158, Japan

Gilbert J. B. Probst, Professor of Management and Organization Theory, University of Geneva, 1211 Geneva 4, Switzerland

Albert Somit, Distinguished Professor, Southern Illinois University, Carbondale, Illinois 62901, USA

Introduction

Magoroh Maruyama

It is often said that we must understand today's economic and political problems in cultural, social, psychological, historical, geographical and other contexts. However, principles and methods of contextual reasoning are not yet well developed despite several waves of attempts over the past four decades. The difficulty is not only methodological but more basically epistemological, involving different mindscape types as discussed in this book.

In the 1950s we saw a surge of interdisciplinary studies continuing into the 1960s. Think tanks, multidisciplinary and interdepartmental institutes, joint appointments, and degree programs became fashionable. At that time the prevailing principles were (a) to put specialists from several fields together to discuss a topic or a problem, (b) to encourage infusion of extradepartmental ideas by hiring persons of other departments part-time or full-time, (c) to offer interdepartmental degree programs by combining courses from many departments, and (d) to set up institutes or departments to study generalized theories. These principles are of the H-type mindscapes, whose universe consists of categories. Books were and still are written with the same principles.

These principles left intact the way of thinking of most of the participants of the activities. Each person brought his or her specialized pieces of information or interpretation to the gathering, and took home what was useful to his or her specialization. In the case of books and degree programs, the situation was worse. Each chapter or each course presented discipline-specific contents and views, and the task of interrelating various chapters and courses was left to the readers and students. On the other hand, general theorists lacked experience in specifics, leaving them to others.

The first three principles tended to become a collage or an encyclopedic catalogue to be used as an indexed reference work, part by part. The fourth principle had another set of problems. It tended to look for universality, analogy, and similarities between various social, biological, and physical processes, ignoring the existence, necessity, and desirability of heterogeneity, and it was prone to standardization, extrapolation, or abstraction without a reality base. In fact, many of the general theorists had no experience with concrete details. They claimed to counteract the reductionism of specialists, but fell into a reductionism of another sort—oversimplification, homogenization, nonempirical fantasy, and wishful normativism. These are also aspects of H-type mindscapes.

In the 1970s and 1980s the interdisciplinary thrust and enthusiasm of the preceding decades gradually died out. Often the decreasing budget was blamed for the decline. However, had the interdisciplinarity taken root in the minds of at least some faculty members, they could have carried on their interdisciplinary thinking even under the budget cuts. Moreover, interdepartmental appointments and courses would have saved money and would have been a better survival strategy, especially under decreasing enrollment. The fact that this route was not taken is a proof that developments in the 1950s and 1960s depended too much on making collections of categorized pieces without altering the way of thinking of each person. In other words, interdisciplinarity had not become intrinsic and endogenous, but remained exotic and exogenous to each person.

In the early 1960s there were several social movements counteracting the predominant "mainstream" H-type hierarchical and homogenistic principles, notably the hippie movement and ethnic minority movements. The hippie movement advocated principles such as "Do your own thing!" and "Grow your own potatoes!" Mushrooming encounter groups created cozy inward-looking enclaves to shut themselves off from the outside world, outside people, and even from one another. They became isolationistic while being heterogenistic. The isolationistic heterogeneity is a characteristic of I-type mindscapes. Many of the ethnic movements had a similar tendency. As we shall see, the H-type and the I-type are actually two sides of the same coin, the latter rising against the former from time to time in history: sophists in ancient Greece, nominalists in medieval Europe, atonal music composers in the mid-20th century.

If the H-type and I-type are two sides of the same coin, there are also other coins. An example is the causal loop logic used in cybernetics, ecology, and econometrics. It is heterogenistic but interactive, not isolationistic. There are several subtypes of it. One is pattern-stabilizing and is called the S-type. Another is pattern-generating, and is called the G-type. There are many other subtypes within each type, as well as many other coins.

This book is based on a G-type principle: heterogenistic, interactive, and pattern-generating. It is not a collection of views from many disciplines. It does not first categorize and then combine. It begins with relations and ends with relations. Each chapter is not only interdisciplinary, but also contextual and relational. S-type and G-type mindscapes are heterogenistic, interactive, contextual, and can deal with complexity without reductionism or theoretical simplification. This book aims at helping the reader develop a contextual way to understand and act in complex situations.

Contextual understanding must be cultivated in several ways: (a) by becoming aware of the relations among seemingly unrelated aspects of human activities such as social interaction patterns, science, aesthetics, business practices, and politics; (b) by looking at a complex situation contextually to generate fresh insights and new interpretations without being bound by existing theories; (c) by having one's feet firmly on the details of the concrete reality of his/her daily activities; (d) by proceeding in one's activities while looking beyond seemingly simple rules; (e) by developing the ability for cross-disciplinary fertilization of concepts without falling into simplifying analogies; and (f) by being wary of reductionistic holism which tends to oversimplification, homogenization, nonempirical constructs, extrapolation, superficial analogy, or wishful normativism.

The six chapters of this book correspond to these six ways of cultivating contextual understanding. All except the last chapter give concrete examples. The first chapter offers examples from urban planning, international business, and other complex activities. The second chapter takes a fresh look at the bewildering economic problems in Argentina. The third brings you to a factory floor in Japan. The fourth presents empirical advice from two management experts of a large Swiss store chain. The fifth illustrates a fruitful cross-fertilization between biology and political science. The sixth is a critical view from a leading French epistemologist. All six chapters are interrelated in a mutually enhancing way, which is characteristic of the G-type mindscapes of the six authors.

As you notice, three of the chapters include examples from business management. This is because business management has become a frontier of complexity requiring contextual thinking. Many other fields are also becoming almost as complex.

In addition to the various social movements mentioned above, the 1960s, 1970s, and 1980s have seen some changes in the attitude of the young generation toward the government and business. In the late 1960s the young generation tended to see both the government and business as "the bad guys," mainly due to the war in Vietnam and the aggravating pollution problems in the United States. The government and business were seen as a huge undifferentiated black box full of evil, conspiracy, and exploitation. This was a result of a simplistic, H-type thinking common to the reductionistic holism then popular among the hippies. In 1969 the government enacted the National Environmental Policy Act, to be implemented by 1972. In the 1970s the government became a slightly better guy in the eyes of the young generation, whereas business continued to be seen as an aggregate of unscrupulous exploiters. Traditionally those in the fields of the humanities and social sciences held business in low esteem without knowing much about it. Many of them tended to think that business consisted of risk-taking investors and bookkeeping accountants who thought about nothing but money. This is another symptom of the reductionistic thinking. They were almost completely unaware that the daily activities of a significant percentage of those in business firms centered around psychological and sociological human relations among employees, interaction patterns and social organization inside the firm, job satisfaction, quality of working life, motivation, and more recently, intercultural communication and culturally different management principles. Recently the young generation has had more realistic contact and experience in the business world and has begun to understand its complexity.

International business has emerged as probably the most complex activity, involving cultures, psychology, sociology, and political science as well as economics. Business is far from being a junkyard for school dropouts and nonintellectuals. It has become a frontier needing those who can think in context and complexity, even though the supply and active use of such human resources are alarmingly lagging behind. But the examples of the problems found in international business management are useful intellectually and, more importantly, epistemologically to those who are in the humanities and social sciences as well as those in engineering and science. The examples help us contextualize and complexify our thinking.

In addition, the first chapter contains many contextual examples from sociology, anthropology, biology, art, and architectural design, and the fifth chapter explores relations between biology and political science. The sixth chapter theoretically summarizes all these concrete examples.

1
Interrelations Among Science, Politics, Aesthetics, Business Management, and Economics

MAGOROH MARUYAMA

Today's complex problems in international economics, business, urban planning, and many other fields require contextual understanding and action. The purpose of this chapter is to illustrate the interrelations among seemingly separate aspects of our life such as science, politics, aesthetics, business management, and economics with concrete and complex examples including multicultural management frictions in international business, governmental projects, and nongovernmental programs; political and economic restructuring currently taking place in East European countries; international debt repayment default problems in Latin America; and, more important, the problems in our own intellectual reorientation and reorganization in coping with them. These problems are ultimately epistemological rather than material and quantitative.

The ability of an individual to effectively deal with multicultural human management frictions, frustrations in working under foreign political and legal constraints, and confusion in facing new international economic changes depends not only on intellectual strength and emotional maturity, but also on cross-epistemological understanding. Many of the managers who are sent to overseas posts from firms renowned for superb human management fail miserably. Physicists who created new theories a decade ago become obstacles to still newer theories. People with excellent knowledge of foreign cultures or scientific paradigms still fail. Their failures stem from the fact that survival in today's world requires a new ability to relate seemingly unrelated aspects of our life, for the task of which our established classificational way of thinking is no longer adequate. We need to make use of new mindscape types (Maruyama, 1979b, 1980). They are epistemological types rather than personality types, value systems, or paradigms.

Mindscape types differ from individual to individual. Firms as well as countries vary in their mainstream mindscape type. Even though all individual types exist in every country, they are modified by cultural, social, corporate, and even intra-firm departmental influences in such a way that in each country, firm, or department, a predominant mainstream type is established, making international, interfirm, and sometimes even interdepartmental interactions difficult. The solution lies in (a) realizing that epistemologically different mindscape types exist, (b) understanding the types other than one's own, and (c) utilizing individually different mindscape types that have been obscured by the mainstream type. This last point is particularly important in discovering the scarce human resources that can serve as a bridge in multicultural, cross-cultural, interfirm, and interdepartmental management and planning.

Until recently, the study of epistemological types has been conducted mainly in two separate fields with two different sets of variables. Psychologists have focused on individual differences in patterns of cognition and/or perception, often in relation to personality characteristics. Research ranged from psychological tests on worldview and personality (Adorno & Sanford, 1950; Rokeach, 1960) and the psychoanalytic bases of choice of theories in physical, biological, and social sciences (Kubie, 1956) and in philosophy (Feuer, 1959), to large-scale statistical testing (Harvey, 1966) and identification of decision-making patterns (Minsky, 1975) as well as unconscious and automatic aspects of such patterns (Kihlstrom, 1987). On the other hand, sociologists and anthropologists have concentrated on social and cultural differences in patterns of cognition, perception, behavior, and causal explanation, often averaging the individual differences within a social group or a culture (see, for example, Camara, 1975; Kluckhohn, 1949; Mannheim, 1929; Mead, 1937; and, to some extent, Kuhn, 1962).

The author has been studying patterns of cognition, perception, conceptualization, design, planning, and decision making from a different direction. In the course of his study of various causal models (Maruyama, 1960, 1963) in physical, biological, and social sciences, it became increasingly evident that the choice of causal model types in research depended on researchers' epistemological types, which were related to their personality characteristics and cultural backgrounds (Maruyama, 1974a). Moreover, differences in epistemological types were found among professionals such as urban and regional planners, engineers, architects, and composers (Maruyama, 1974b, 1976, 1977, 1978a, 1978b, 1979a, 1979b, 1980, 1981, 1982, 1984a, 1984b, 1985a, 1985b, 1985c, 1986a, 1986b, 1987a, 1987b). The author developed the mindscape theory (Maruyama, 1979b, 1980). Independently, in his voluminous statistical data, Harvey (1966) identified four epistemological types, which in 1975 were matched with Maruyama's mindscape types. It turned out that Harvey's types I, II, and IV were practically identical with Maruyama's types H, I and G respectively, even though Harvey's type III and Maruyama's S-type were considerably different.

The mindscape theory may appear to be a typology. However, its purpose and use lie in interrelating seemingly separate aspects of human activities such as organizational structure, policy formulation, decision process, architectural design, criteria of beauty, choice of theories, cosmology, etc. It is relational rather than classificational.

Mindscape types vary from individual to individual and are numerous. However, four types are found most frequently, together with mixtures among themselves and with other types. The types are partly innate and partly learned. Different cultures and professions exercise different pressures for or against some types in the process of acculturation, socialization, ostracism, marginalizatioin, etc. Individuals also exercise self-selection, internalization, sublimation, attrition, alienation, repression, identification, etc.

Some selected characteristics of the four most frequent types are shown in Table 1. As can be seen, the mindscape types are quite different from the Jungian, Jaspersian, and other psychological typologies. They represent diverse epistemological metatypes. Furthermore, these mindscape characteristics provide a link between seemingly separate activities such as decision process, choice of criteria of beauty, and choice of science theories. It is also important to point out that these

TABLE 1. Characteristics of four mindscape types.

H-type	I-type	S-type	G-type
homogenist	heterogenist	heterogenist	heterogenizing
universalist	individualist	mutualist	mutualizing
hierarchical	isolationist	interactive	interactive
classifying	randomizing	contextual	contextualizing
eternal	temporary	pattern-maintaining	pattern-generating
sequential	no order	simultaneous	simultaneous
competitive	uniquing	cooperative	cogenerative
zero-sum	negative-sum	positive-sum	positive-sum
unity by similarity	independence	mutual gain by diversity	mutual gain by diversity
identity	identity	relation	relating
specialization	specialization	convertibility, job rotation	convertibility, job rotation
opposition	separation	absorption	absorption
tension	indifference	continuity	flow
extension	caprice	stability	development
one truth	subjectivity	polyocular	polyocular

four types do *not* line up on one scale, *nor* do they fit in a two-by-two table. They are more like the four corners of a tetrahedron (a pyramid-like shape with a triangular bottom). If anything, H and I are two sides of one coin, and S and G are two sides of a different coin. However, the line H-I is *not* parallel to the line S-G. Therefore they cannot be put in a two-by-two table.

The preceding list of the characteristics of four mindscape types serves as a sort of projective test used in psychology. One can tell the mindscape type of a person by the way he or she reacts to the list: (a) if the person notices that the list is not exhaustive and the categories are not mutually exclusive, and tries to make it exhaustive and mutually exclusive, then he or she is of the H-type; (b) if the person rejects the list as completely irrelevant, then he or she is of the I-type; (c) if the person interprets the list as changeable depending on situations and circumstances, then the person is of the S-type or G-type.

Some Concrete Examples

Business management principles and practices vary from firm to firm and from country to country, depending on the mindscape type predominant in each. Similarly economic policies vary from country to country depending on its mindscape type. Some examples follow.

The Concept of Employee

(H) Hire those who fit the job descriptions. The employee is evaluated on specialized performances. Promote vertically along the line of specialization. In some cases job rotation may be practiced for limited purposes. For example, in Sweden, some factories rotate their employees (a) to prepare human spare parts that can replace sick workers, (b) to relieve the fatigue of specific muscles or eyes, and (c) to counteract boredom.

(I) Hire unusual talents instead of using job descriptions. Let each person develop in his/her own way. This principle is practiced by two types of firms: (a) entrepreneurial firms, for example those found in Silicon Valley; and (b) firms large enough to be able to afford basic research, for example DuPont.

(S) Hire on the basis of the ability for contextual thinking rather than specialization, and with a consideration for future potential instead of skills acquired in the past. In many Japanese firms, job rotation is extensive across departmental boundaries for the following purposes: (a) The employee can experience fellow workers' jobs and can feel mentally connected with them. This principle of connectedness is manifested also in the Japanese concept of architectural space as discussed before (Maruyama, 1981). It is also an aspect of aidaschaft (Maruyama, 1984a). (b) The employee becomes able to see the same situation from different points of view, i.e., acquires polyocular vision. (c) The employee can understand each job in the context of other jobs and become proficient at quality control and making suggestions for overall improvement. This is the Japanese meaning of quality control, whereas American factories strive to attain quality by tight inspection. Also each employee becomes capable of correcting errors made by others. This will be discussed further under the heading of responsibility. To accomplish these three purposes, most large firms in Japan require new entrants, with or without a university degree or engineering degree, to spend 2 or 3 years in the assembly line, at retail store counters, and at repair service runs. Throughout their careers they are rotated through many departments. Often an extensive job rotation is a prerequisite for promotion. Later in their careers, they often visit the "bottom" to spend time with workers. Many of the prefectural and municipal governments practice similar job rotations.

(G) Most of the inventions in Japanese firms are made by teams, consisting of heterogeneous abilities and skills, as will be discussed. The insight and foresight of managers in combining heterogeneous individuals are crucial. Many of them are capable of the task because they have been extensively job-rotated as in (S) (Maruyama, 1989a).

Responsibility

(H) Responsibility is neatly divided among individuals without overlapping. To go beyond one's responsibility is considered to be trespassing, for example making a suggestion for another department.

(I) Each person sets his/her own sphere of responsibility.

(S) Responsibility is overlapping. For example, if there are five people in a group, each takes 100% responsibility for the work of the entire group, with the result that a total of 500% is taken. In practical terms, each worker in an assembly line is capable of correcting errors that have been made by someone preceding him/her. This results in high productivity. For example, in the assembly lines of a car manufacturer in Sweden, the unit in which an error was found must be taken out of the line and sent back to where the error was made. In modern car manufacturing, different types of cars are mixed in sequence on the assembly line: one car to go to France with yellow headlights, next car for England for left-hand driving, etc. Parts that are fed into the assembly line must also be sequenced accordingly. Taking one unit out of the sequence involves readjustment of the parts lines and is costly. On each spot on the assembly line, the work is paced to leave extra seconds between units. The Swedish workers do knitting or reading to pace the waiting period (so many knots or so many lines of text until the next unit arrives). The Japanese workers keep checking and double-checking the unit on which he/she has just finished working.

(G) Similar to (S).

Worker Standardization and De-standardization

(H) It is democratic, economical, and efficient to treat all employees equally, regardless of color, sex, individual habits, or circumstances. This principle is homogenistic and standardizing.

(I) It is democratic, economical, and efficient to let each worker work at his/her own pace and in his/her own way, independent from others.

(S) Positive use of individual differences by combining them in a mutually beneficial way. Japanese workers like to work in a group. As in the Japanese garden design and floral art, the individual idiosyncrasies are maximally used because the group members know one another well. In any country, a good sports team does the same.

(G) Same as (S).

Invention

(H) Inventions are made by individuals.

(I) Same as (H).

(S) See (G).

(G) Mathematician Stanislaw Ulam (1960) proved that new information arises in interactions among heterogeneous elements, which is different from new combinations of old elements, i.e., genuine creativity is possible by interaction between ideas in one person's mind or among many persons. H-type and I-type mindscapes can consider inventions as arising from interactions of ideas in one person's head. S-type and G-type mindscapes generate inventions by interactions among heterogeneous individuals. Many of the inventions in Japan are done by groups. It must be pointed out that the number of patents in electronics by Japanese have exceeded that of Americans (Gregory, 1986). There are several well-documented case studies of Japanese inventions (Uchihashi, 1982). An example was the first wristwatch using a quartz electronic resonant circuit by Seiko, which defeated Swiss watches in timekeeping accuracy in a Swiss competition held in 1967. The authorities of this time-honored Neuchâtel competition panicked and did not publish the result (Uchihashi, 1982), and discontinued the competition in subsequent years. Prior to miniaturization, the first quartz clock that still used vacuum tubes instead of transistors was so big that it had to be transported on a pickup truck. Seiko achieved miniaturization by several methods. One is to cut quartz in a zigzag way to compress into a small space the length needed for desired resonance frequency. By combining quartz experts who did not know how to cut quartz with jewelry makers, Seiko could put the quartz in the wristwatch. Another example was elimination, in the 1950s, of derailing problems of high-speed trains by combining aircraft technologies to eliminate spontaneous resonant vibration, which led to the creation of the bullet train. The traditional train engineers believed that the derailments were caused by crooked rails. But aircraft engineers thought that trains may get a resonant vibration regardless of how straight the rails were. It was decided to conduct experiments with models. For railway engineers, the models were to run on model tracks. But the aircraft engineers used the wind-tunnel concept, in which the models stayed still and the rails moved on a very large rotating wheel. In this system it was easy to measure and control the swaying of rails. The experiments proved that the trains vibrated at some specific speeds. (Maruyama, 1985c, 1989a).

Economic Policies

(H) Change a key variable to affect the national economy. The variable chosen depends on the theoretical school of the economists. Monetarists choose money supply or interest rate (by changing the reserve ratio or by selling and buying securities). Keynesians choose government expenditure as investment to stimulate economic activities. Supply-siders choose consumers' disposable income (by reducing taxes). In all cases, causal loops are not discussed systematically and comprehensively. Similarly, some political scientists consider a small number of institutions to be the cause, such as the social security system, the individual savings system, etc.

(I) If everybody produces what he/she consumes, there is no economic problem ("Grow your own potatoes"). Economic interactions among people are the cause of the problems.

(S) The economic system is inherently self-stabilizing or cyclic. Disturbances are due to "exogenous" (noneconomic) influences such as government interference, war, etc. (As we see below, this assumption is mathematically incorrect. However, most economists adhere to this assumption like a superstition.) Laissez-faire is the best policy.

(G) The economic system contains both change-amplifying and change-counteracting loops (Maruyama, 1963, 1986b; Myrdal, 1944, 1957). Economic policy failures occur when change-amplifying causal loops are ignored. For example, the existing economic theories are still unable to determine why the Great Depression of the 1930s occurred. A good economic policy consists in creating and making use of the loops that amplify beneficial effects, and reducing or breaking harmful and counterproductive loops, because the economic system is *not* self-stabilizing.

International Trade Policies

(H) International trade is a zero-sum game. One country's gain is another's loss. For a country to gain, it must make others lose. Therefore, reduce imports. Import restriction war ensues.

(I) International trade is a negative-sum game: all sides lose by trading. It is better for each country to be self-sufficient without export or import. This fallacious reasoning is one of the causes of the failure of the Japanese agricultural policy, in which the costly subsidies resulted in inefficiency of production, resulting in a rice price six times higher than the international average, and beef often ten times the international average. Another cause is the consumers' fallacious zero-sum belief that their sacrifice by paying the high price is benefiting the farmers. Labor and materials are wasted in inefficient production, storage, and distribution systems. The gain to the farmers is far less than the loss to the consumers (Maruyama, 1987a).

(G) All countries should increase exports to one another, instead of reducing imports. This will make the international velocity of money (speed of circulation of money) greater, increase the speed of economic activities, and can increase the gross national product (GNP) of all countries. The United States can increase its exports by adapting product design to foreign markets (Maruyama, 1987b). Most Americans assume that the products that are good for Americans are also good for foreigners. This is an incorrect assumption. The use patterns, consumer preferences, and user habits vary from country to country. The product design must be adapted accordingly. One problem is that for most American firms, the main market is domestic. They are unfamiliar with foreign markets and unwilling to change the product designs for foreign markets. On the other hand, firms in countries such as Sweden and Switzerland, whose domestic market is very small, are more used to export product design adaptation. The Japanese want to buy a wider variety of American products, but very few American firms are interested. More than 30 states in the United States have representatives in Japan, but their main purpose is to invite Japanese firms to open factories in their states, *not* to promote exports. This will help the balance of payment, which includes investment, but does not improve trade balance.

Concept of Investment and Return in International Aid

(H) England developed the concept and practice of investment and return during its Industrial Revolution. This can be called "manufacturism." The economic aid given by North American and West European countries is based on this manufacturism assumption of investment for return. Furthermore, it is assumed that money is a universal instrument of transaction, i.e., anything can be bought with money. According to this second assumption, to provide money is to provide a free choice of what to obtain with it. Policy makers of the H-type in North America and Western Europe tend to extrapolate these two assumptions to other countries. However, these assumptions are invalid in many Latin American and Asian countries. As we will see below, investment may be unrelated to return, and there may be commodities and services that cannot be bought with money. An example is mainland China where investment is allocated without much concern with its return. An enterpreneur in such a system is a person skilled at obtaining budget allocations, not a person capable of attaining a high return-on-investment ratio. In this sense the entrepreneur in the Chinese system resembles the grantsman among North American academics who is skilled at obtaining grants. Grants do not have to be repaid. In joint ventures with foreign firms, Chinese entreprises tend to regard foreign investments as grants. If deficits occur, one seeks additional grants. Furthermore, there are many commodities and services that money cannot buy. For example, in mainland China an apartment is provided to a family with almost no payment. But one cannot buy or rent an additional apartment with money. The socialist system in China is of the H-type. This means that even within H-type social systems, the two assumptions may be invalid. On the other hand, there are also cases in non-H social systems where the two assumptions are valid. Therefore we *cannot* say that the assumptions themselves are of the H-type. But the tendency to *extrapolate* them is of the H-type (Maruyama, 1989b).

(I) While England developed manufacturism, Spain extracted gold and silver from South America and built her wealth without manufacturing. The economic practice was based on windfall gain. Investment was needed for exploration, military conquest, and colonization, but the gain was unrelated to or disproportional to the amount of investment. We can call this development "extractionism." By now, extraction of gold and silver is no longer a major economic activity in Latin America. But the initial trend can be amplified and/or maintained by causal loops long after the disappearance of the initial kick (Maruyama, 1961b, 1963). In Latin America, international loan can be regarded as a windfall gain that does not have to be repaid. If a repayment is urged, it can be refinanced with another windfall gain (Maruyama, 1989b).

(S) In Indonesia, it is better to have one taxi driver than three ditch diggers among 20 relatives, because the income of a person is distributed to his/her relatives. When there is an adequate way to distribute income, technology-intensive methods of production are better than labor-intensive methods even under high unemployment conditions. We can call such a practice "sharism." In countries where there is no adequate income distribution system, sharism can be approximated by everyone working part-time. In both cases, unemployed hours or free hours from part-time employment can be used for skill upgrading. Under sharism, a loan from a foreign country can be interpreted as an international sharing that does not require a rigid repayment schedule, but in a long-range view the recipient will eventually give a loan to less wealthy countries. This can be called "cascade aid."

(G) East European countries are under rapid political and economic reorganization. In several of these countries, many persons who had experienced the presocialist days are still alive. But the younger generations have had no experience of working in a free market system that requires high productivity, efficiency, individual initiative, inventiveness, and serious work habits. In the USSR, where the socialist regime began 70 years ago, there is practically no one alive who had worked in a free market system. These conditions in Eastern Europe and the USSR require double tasks: (a) to acquire skills and expertise in management in a free market system, and (b) to avoid superficial copying of the methods developed in other countries, and to develop new management principles and methods compatible with the culture of each country. Free market countries have made many mistakes in cross-cultural management. Transfer or imposition of exogenous management principles and methods that did not take the cultural differences into consideration failed. In recent years the workers in Eastern Europe and the USSR had become accustomed to receiving their income without being productive. Officials had come to depend on bribes. Bribing became more rampant than in free market countries. In a free market system, one has to maintain some level of productivity and cannot live entirely on bribes. But in a non–free market system, one can. When a free market system will be introduced, there will be much resistance from workers who would rather not work hard, and from officials and managers who have become used to living on bribes. How to engineer the transition politically and managerially is a very difficult task. At the same time, how to revive the older tradition of each country, enhance it with new technology, and use it as the basis of a new political and economic development is another formidable task. Furthermore, developments in several countries must be coordinated without loss of each country's uniqueness and making use of the cultural differences among them. All these tasks require a high degree of G-type inventiveness. G-type mindscapes are needed not only in Eastern Europe and the USSR but also in mainland China and Latin America where dependism and extractionism prevail (Maruyama, 1989b, 1990a).

Mindscape Theory Has Developed From Interdisciplinary Activities

Now that we have seen some examples of the relationships between mindscape types, business management principles, and economic policies, let us look into the mindscape theory further, which elucidates the interactions among science, politics, aesthetics, and business management.

The mindscape theory in the present form has developed in practical fields of urban planning (Maruyama, 1973, 1974b), outer space community design (Maruyama, 1976, 1984b), and international business management (Maruyama, 1984a, 1985a, 1986b). However, it has its origin in the study of causal metatypes in physical sciences (Maruyama, 1960, 1963): H-type corresponds to Newtonian physics; I-type corresponds to 19th century thermodynamics and 20th century Shannonian mathematical theory of information; S-type corresponds to the first cybernetics of the 1940s and 1950s based on change-counteracting causal loops; G-type corresponds to the second cybernetics which began in the 1960s, based on change-amplifying causal loops.

In the early 1970s I was in urban planning, and had to sort out arguments in public hearings. It became evident that the same slogan such as "small is beautiful" or "decentralization" can be advocated on several epistemologically different grounds (Maruyama, 1979b), and apparent agreements may stand on undetected disagreements that later cause problems. Between 1972 and 1975, I identified several frequent types and used sometimes three (Maruyama, 1974a) and sometimes five (Maruyama, 1977) types in my analysis. By early 1976, I settled on four frequent types.

Then in the summer of 1976 I met O. J. Harvey while attending a biological conference at the University of Colorado. He told me that he had been giving psychological tests to university students over several decades and identified four frequent epistemological types. He and I were both surprised by the fact that his type I, type II, and type IV were amazingly compatible with my H-type, I-type, and G-type, respectively, and that their statistical distribution that he found was very similar to what I found among American professionals and academics, even though different from my findings in other cultures. Before I met Harvey, I had been thinking that someday I ought to determine if mindscape types could be identified in some large-scale statistical data because my findings were not statistically constructed, even though they included a large number of individuals. Harvey's data were exactly the kind of thing I was looking for. I was happy to see that Harvey's findings supported the existence of mindscape types, even though his types and mine were not completely identical.

Harvey characterized his four types, which he called "systems," as follows (Harvey, 1966): (a) System I: high absolutism and closedness of beliefs; high evaluativeness; high positive dependence on representatives of institutional authority; high identification with social roles and status positions; high conventionality; high ethnocentrism. (b) System II: deep feelings of uncertainty, distrust of authority, rejection of the more socially approved guidelines to action accompanied by lack of alternative referents; psychological vacuum; rebellion against social prescriptions; avoidance of dependency on God and tradition. (c) System III: manipulating of people through dependency upon them; fairly high skills in effecting desired outcomes in his world through the techniques of having others do it for him; autonomous internal standards, especially in the social sphere; some positive ties to the prevailing social norms. (d) System IV: high perceived self-worth despite momentary frustrations and deviation from the norm; highly differentiated and integrated cognitive structure; flexible, creative, and relative in thought and action; internal standards that are independent of external criteria, in some cases coinciding with social definitions and in others not.

In describing the four types, Harvey uses personality characteristics more, whereas I used cognitive characteristics more. However, his and mine are parallel notions that are quite compatible. This compatibility becomes clearer as I discuss more specifics of the mindscape types, even though some differences will remain.

Here again, these differences serve as a projective test in psychology. If the reader is bothered by them and tries to make the two schemes completely compatible, then he or she is of the H-type. On the other hand, if the reader finds the differences interesting and useful in the sense of binocular or polyocular vision, and can live with them comfortably, then he or she is of the S-type or G-type.

Another point of interest is that Harvey's system 1 is reminiscent of the F-scale (Adorno & Sanford, 1950). In fact, the stimuli he uses in his psychological tests are verbal statements similar to those used in the F-scale. However, whereas the F-scale rates the test subjects between the two poles of high authoritarianism and low authoritarianism, Harvey ended up with four distinct types that cannot be lined up on one scale. As can be understood from the following discussion on mindscape characteristics, the one-scale methodology, the two-by-two table methodology, the m-by-n matrix methodology, etc., are all based on an H-type mindscape. An important point is that Harvey does *not* attempt to put his four types on one scale, nor in a two-by-two table. This indicates that Harvey himself is probably not of the H-type. Can we say that Adorno and Sanford were of an H-type? I do not think we can. I have never met Adorno, but I have known Sanford for many years, and I know that he is not of the H-type. Then why did he use a one-scale method? I think it was a matter of the Zeitgeist under which the F-scale study was undertaken. It was the time of Hitler's anti-Semitism. Adorno and Sanford wanted to know if Americans were susceptible to Hitler-type anti-Semitism. They constructed the F-scale to discover personality characteristics that were prone to ideologies similar to anti-Semitism.

This brings us to the importance of sociocultural circumstances as an overlay to the individual mindscape. It complicates our analysis of mindscape types.

With these preliminary remarks, let us now look at some of the characteristics of mindscape types.

Selected Characteristics of Mindscape Types

The list of mindscape characteristics is quite long, and in fact, there are several lists that I published for use in different academic and professional fields, for example: (a) science theory formulation, hypotheses-making, and research methodology (Maruyama, 1978b, 1980); (b) causal models (Maruyama, 1960, 1963, 1982, 1986b); (c) biology (Maruyama, 1977); (d) sociology (Maruyama, 1978a); (e) information theory (Maruyama, 1965, 1972); (f) communications (Maruyama, 1974a, 1979a); (g) urban planning (Maruyama, 1973, 1974b, 1979b); (h) architecture (Maruyama, 1981); (i) outer space community design (Maruyama, 1976, 1984b); (j) international business management (Maruyama, 1984a, 1985a); and (k) international marketing (Maruyama, 1985b, 1985c).

It is not possible to present a complete list here. Consequently, only some selected characteristics are shown below.

Knowledge

(H) Knowledge of general rules is higher than knowledge of specifics. Objectivity exists independently from the perceiver. Differences in perception are due to errors, and are useless. Objective understanding is attained by quantitative measurement.

(I) Knowledge consists of specific pieces of information needed for each activity.

(S) Knowledge is attained by polyocular vision. In the binocular vision, the differences in the two images enable the brain to compute the third dimension invisible to both eyes. Similarly in the polyocular vision, the differences in perception by many persons are indispensable in computing the dimensions no one can see. (Note: "Dimension" does *not* mean size, scale, angle, or part.)

(G) Similar to (S).

Understanding and Meaning

(H) Characteristics include (a) to rank-order, classify, and categorize; (b) to perceive and understand sequentially; (c) to look for regularity and common features; (d) to determine meaning by the category and subcategory to which the object or concept belongs; the meaning is inherent in it; and (e) perception strives for precision.

(I) To distinguish and isolate phenomena, each of which is unique and unrelated to others.

(S) Characteristics include (a) to look at interrelations; (b) to see simultaneously; (c) to recognize the diversity among the elements, and to think of mutually beneficial interactions among them; (d) to recognize that meaning exists in interrelations and contexts, and is *not* inherent in the element. When the relation and contextual situation are known, the meaning is known; and (e) perception strives for polyocularity.

(G) Similar to (S), except (d), which can be stated: Relations and contexts as well as elements can change, and therefore new meanings arise. Multiple meanings occur, and the possibility of multiple interpretations enables innovations and growth.

Human Values

(H) Values can be rank-ordered from the highest to the lowest (Maslow, 1954). Furthermore, the obtained ranking is valid for all cultures because human nature is universal. Values can be classified into neat categories. Universally valid scales of "quality of life" can be constructed and applied to all individuals and all cultures. Personal integrity consists in adhering to higher values regardless of the situation and the context.

(I) Each person has his or her own value system, and each value is independent of other values. The meaning of "quality of life" varies from individual to individual. Personal integrity consists in adhering to one's own value system regardless of what others say or think.

(S) Values are interrelated and cannot be separated into independent categories or rank-ordered. The meaning of each value depends on contexts and cultures, and cannot be universally defined. How a person behaves or should behave is determined mostly by his or her relations with others, i.e., by the social situation and context. Likewise, the person's opinion is a contextual opinion, neither an abstract categorical principle nor an individually isolated point of view that disregards interpersonal context. Personal integrity consists of behavior and opinion that reflect the social situation and context. This is often misinterpreted as inconsistency, dishonesty, or deception by those who have an H-type or an I-type mindscape.

(G) Similar to (S). However, values interact and generate new values and new meanings. Values, needs, and meanings are redefined as new contexts arise. Personal integrity consists in inventing new patterns of interactive behavior that generate mutual benefit in new situations and contexts.

Concept of Heterogeneity

(H) Heterogeneity is due to random fluctuations, accidents, errors, abnormality, or deviance. It is the source of conflicts. It is unnecessary and undesirable except in resource diversification. If all species ate the same food, there would be food shortage. If some species were not eaten, there would be accumulation of corpses. Heterogeneity is useful in resource diversification (a zero-sum relation).

(I) Each person is different and independent from others. Heterogeneity is basic and useful, especially in risk dispersion in case of sudden environmental changes (a negative-sum relation).

(S) Heterogeneity enables cooperation and mutual help. It is necessary and desirable. It is the source of peace (a positive-sum relation).

(G) Heterogeneity is mutually beneficial. Heterogeneity increases in biological, social, cultural, and epistemological evolution, and makes mutually beneficial combinations of new types of elements (a positive-sum relation).

Beauty in Design, and Creativity

(H) Unity is achieved by repetition, regularity, symmetry, and similarity. Dominant themes are reflected in subordinate themes. Examples are Gothic and Islamic architecture, traditional Italian and French gardens, Chinese interior decoration, and Japanese architecture of the Yamato period influenced by Korean culture. Regular geometric shapes such as spheres and squares, as well as arithmetic proportions in music were considered beautiful by Parmenides and Pythagoras. Da Vinci went so far as to fit human body proportions into squares and circles, and North American art teachers teach students to draw an animal or human body by decomposing it into a series of circles and ovals.

(I) Beauty is random, capricious, and haphazard. Some modern European music composers and architects use randomness as an alternative to repetition. Schoenberg went as far as systematizing the randomization in his twelve-tone techniques. But it is a fallacy to consider randomness as a source of creativity (Maruyama, 1974a). Creativity consists in generating new patterns and new structures, and is the opposite of randomness. See more under (G).

(S) Avoid repetition of similar elements and combine diverse elements into a harmony. The interrelations between heterogeneous elements are perceived to maintain a pattern in such a way that if an element is displaced a few centimeters, the design looks less beautiful. Examples are some, but not all, of the Japanese gardens and floral designs, especially those inspired by Yayoi principles (Maruyama, 1981). Watsuji (1935) attributed the Japanese preference for irregular shapes to the fact that in Japan, where both the tropical monsoon climate and the northern winter climate meet, floods, typhoons, and avalanches break tree branches and other elements in inconsistent ways, resulting in landscapes consisting of irregular shapes. Furthermore, the Japanese farmers who spent most of their labor on coping with weeds, insects, birds, animals, floods, and droughts, considered themselves as a part of the interactions in the ecosystem, and cultivated the sense of harmony of diverse elements. On the other hand, in Europe the seasonal changes are more orderly and predictable: storms are less severe, insects and weeds are less ferocious, and animals and birds are more easily controlled. Watsuji considered this to be the reason for Europeans' admiration of regular forms and rhythms as beautiful. There is a superficial resemblance between the English gardens and the Japanese gardens. However, the Japanese garden designs are based on very complex and elaborate rules of interrelations among the elements (Maruyama, 1981). In Dutch tulip gardens, flowers are used to form color masses like carpets, in which the individuality of each flower disappears. In Japanese gardens, flowers and flower trees tend to be more scattered, and occupy individually meaningful positions in relation to others. In floral art, interactions among the heterogeneous composition elements enhance the individuality of each element.

(G) Increasingly diverse elements generate new harmony. Make designs for simultaneously multiple as well as changing interpretations, as in Japanese haiku poetry and some garden and floral art

(Maruyama, 1981). Some old Greek architects (for example Pergamon) and European painters such as Picasso and music composers such as Stravinsky show many G-type characteristics. Deliberate incompleteness to enable addition of new elements and changes is often used. Creativity is possible due to interactions among heterogeneous ideas. In 19th century thermodynamics and in more recent Shannonian information theory (Shannon, 1949), structures were to decay but could not be created, because both assumed that the most probable state inside an isolated system is random distribution of independent events, each behaving with its own probability. For example, random winds on a beach cannot create a sand castle. However, if there are interactions among the elements within an isolated system (for example, if sand grains are able to interact), patterns and structures can be generated (Maruyama, 1960, 1963). Mathematician and logician Stanislaw Ulan (1960) formulated that the amount of information needed to describe the finished pattern is greater than that needed to describe the interactive rules in many cases. Mathematically, this means that genuinely new patterns are created, not just new combinations of old patterns. In thermodynamic terms, entropy can decrease.

Architectural Space and Mass

(H) Space is defined as something between masses. Space is a transparent mass with shape, volume, boundary, identity, and specialized function, such as a dining room or a bedroom, and is occupied by specialized furniture. The house separates humans from the environment. Space opposes mass. Many spaces oppose one another. Masses also oppose one another. Tension exists between points. For example, in medieval Rome the seven obelisks erected by a Pope created spatial tension and generated streets to connect them. Two points may define a shaft that becomes extended, as when a queen built a small house outside the city wall of old Paris. When the city expanded, another house was built outside the new city wall. The two points generated a shaft that later became the Champs Élysées. Edge lines and wall surfaces of a building may also be extended to generate shafts of space. Thus the principles of opposition, tension, and extension characterize traditional European spatial design.

(I) Each space and each object is unrelated to others. One form of this principle is the "lego approach" to house design whereby the architect provides the parts that are then assembled to meet individual needs.

(S) Spaces are connected and flow into one another. In the traditional Japanese house, partitions between rooms as well as much of the outer shell of the building can be removed. One can sit in the house and hear the birds and smell the flowers outside. Objects in space represent the quality of the space and do not oppose space. Since objects represent the same space quality, they do not oppose one another. Each room in the house is convertible to many functions: a bedroom at night, a dining room at meal times, and a playing room at other times. Furniture is removed and stored away. Connectedness and convertibility characterize space and object. (As will be seen shortly, the same applies to the concept of the individual, and the concept of an employee.) In some designs, space is a miniature universe and represents the phenomena and processes of the universe, for example tea ceremony rooms, some gardens, and floral art. Note that in contrast, most of the ancient Greek philosophers were preoccupied with "substances" such as fire, air, earth, and water. Even motion was considered to be caused by a power substance that penetrated into things like a car driver.

(G) Space is for activity and interaction with the environment. Space is thought of as around something, for example around a rock or a grove, instead of between things. Space is open outward and contrasts with the enclosed space of H-mindscapes, and the outside-absorbing space of S-mindscape.

The Concept of the Individual

(H) The concept of the individual has many parallels with the concept of space as shown above. In H-type mindscapes, the individual has boundary, identity, and specialization, fits in a category and successively smaller subcategories, and occupies a position in a hierarchy. He can be defined in terms of the category, subcategories, specialization, and hierarchical position.

(I) Uniqueness is independent of others.

(S) The individual is a node of interrelations with others around him/her. Each has a special way and meaning in relating with others, which becomes his/her individuality. Without such relations, there is no individuality. For example, young Japanese people tend to form groups. In each group, the individual fills a special function such as a car expert, a camera expert, a music expert, etc., for the purpose of being useful to other members and for being appreciated by them (Maruyama, 1985b). There is no absolute leader: each becomes a leader for specific activities. This type of individuality is others-oriented: the specialization is developed to fill the needs of the group. Furthermore, it is convertible: it is easily changed when needs change. Such a concept of the individual as a node of relations with others has been named "aidaschaft" (Maruyama, 1984a) in contrast to gemeinschaft and gesellschaft.

(G) Similar to (S) with the following differences. In (G), one must be useful as an explorer, path finder, and innovator. Each collects new information, checks on new trends, etc. There is a large market to meet this need of young people: there are small stores, small restaurants, etc., purposely inconspicuous, camouflaged as ordinary houses or something else, located in hidden alleys, that keep changing their merchandise, interior decoration, etc., to give the young people the excitement of discovery (Maruyama, 1985b). The merchandise is not classified neatly in shelves, but is mixed and piled up in heaps. These stores are located on the periphery of busy areas.

Cause-Effect Relations

(H) Two things cannot cause each other. Cause-effect relations may be deterministic or probabilistic. Many things can jointly or separately cause one thing. One thing may cause many other things at the same time. But there are no causal loops.

(I) Random distribution of independent events, each behaving with its own probability, is most natural and probable. Nonrandom patterns and structures are improbable, and tend to decay.

(S) Many things can cause one another through short or long causal loops. But this does not imply that everything causes everything else. Causal loop interactions maintain a pattern of heterogeneity. Deviations from the pattern are corrected by mutual interaction. The interactive causality can be probabilistic or deterministic. There are two subtypes in the S-type causal loops: in one, interactions asymptotically converge to a stabilized pattern of heterogeneity; in the other, the interactions produce periodic cycles due to time lag. In both cases, dissimilar initial conditions may end up with the same result.

(G) Things can cause one another through short or long causal loops. Interactions amplify change and generate greater heterogeneity (Maruyama, 1960, 1963). There are three subtypes. One consists of interactions that generate mutually beneficial relations among the heterogeneous elements, survive as a viable system, and raise the level of sophistication of the system. The second consists of those interactions in which some elements develop mutually beneficial relations, while others fail and die. The third is a nonviable subtype in which either the change takes place too fast to enable the elements to develop mutual adaptation, or harmful change is amplified beyond control. The interactive causality can be deterministic or probabilistic. In all cases a very small initial kick can be amplified to produce a disproportionally large change. Therefore, similar initial conditions may produce very dissimilar results.

Hypothesis-Making

(H) Choose a variable of your interest (dependent variable). Choose another variable (independent variable) that seems to cause or influence the first. State as a hypothesis: the latter affects the former. It is assumed that similar conditions produce similar results. Therefore, if results are dissimilar, the conditions must be proportionally dissimilar. Trace the differences back to the conditions. (For example, if identical twins have become different, it is hypothesized that something in the environment, the food, the social influence, etc., was different.) It does not occur to H-mindscapes that two variables may cause each other directly or through other variables. Consequently the difference is assumed to exist in the "independent variable." As will be shown in (G), this may be attacking a straw man.

(I) Each variable acts independently. Therefore, there is no cause-effect hypothesis.

(S) Processes that began in dissimilar conditions may asymptotically converge to a pattern, or go in cycles. Look for causal loops that produced the equilibrium or periodicity. Note that the focus is on loops, not on variables.

(G) Processes that began in similar conditions may produce very dissimilar results. Look for change-amplifying loops. In contrast to the H-type hypothesis, the "blame" for the difference is put on the loop, not on any variable, which may be a straw man.

Evolution

(H) The "strongest" survives in competition. All civilizations follow the same path of evolution. Therefore, if two civilizations are different, one is more advanced and the other is more primitive or childlike. White Americans and Europeans are the most advanced. Homo sapiens is the most advanced of all animals. Less advanced should serve the more advanced. Society consists of leaders and followers. Evolution partly depends on mate selection. Among animals, mate selection is based on optimal or supernormal characteristics. Evolution progresses in the direction of characteristics selected in mating and by external pressure. All individuals prefer the same characteristics in mating. Therefore, there is a unified, homogeneous direction of evolution. Or the most average is considered the most beautiful (Langlois & Roggmann, 1990) and therefore may be preferred in mate selection. In human history, major changes are made by heroes, discoveries, and inventions, or by natural, biological, or man-made disasters. Therefore, changes in cultural evolution and human history occur in leaps and jumps.

(I) Evolution is due to random changes. Whatever happens to get established perpetuates itself until another random change wipes it out. Stability is punctuated by sudden random changes in unpredictable directions, which are followed again by stability. Evolution is haphazard and has no coherent direction. Random influences can make established structures decay little by little, but they are not likely to accumulate in a consistent direction so as to form a new structure. Consequently, the emergence of a new form must occur in a leap, such as a sudden genetic change due to exposure to radioactivity.

(S) Evolution is a result of interactions among heterogeneous elements. For a given local condition (size of space, energy supply, temperature, types of nonorganic materials available, etc.) evolution will either proceed toward a stable configuration of interactions with a stabilized number of species and a stabilized number of individuals in each species, or go in repetitive, periodic cycles. When the local conditions change, a new configuration arises. Existing cultures are a result of a long evolutionary process. Each culture fits its local condition and has attained a stable internal configuration that is satisfactory and perfect and should not be disturbed. Changes are due to influences from outside or occasional inventions within the culture. Cultures tend to remain stable, occasionally changing stepwise.

(G) Interactions continuously generate heterogeneity and new patterns of mutually beneficial relations among heterogeneous elements. The development may be gradual or rapid. Changes need not occur in leaps; usually they occur continuously and gradually. However, leaps may occur because of either very rapid change or the exceeding of a threshold. Since "kicks" in various directions may be amplified by causal loops, there are many possible directions of evolution, even within the same local condition. Mate selection may be based on rare characteristics (Ehrman, 1972; Ehrman & Probber, 1978; Watanabe & Kawanishi, 1979); there are no best characteristics. Fruit fly females prefer minority males; if you present them a mixture of Type A and Type B males, the females prefer whichever happens to be a minority. This leads to heterogenization within the species. Evolution does not stop; if some external limits are reached, either new forms may develop to alter the nature of the internal configurations or some device may be created to change the external limits, for example, moving into outer space.

(Comment) The three different assumptions regarding mate selection lead to very different, almost opposing view of evolution. The sociobiologists' assumption of optimal characteristics and the assumption of the average as the most beautiful by Langlois and Roggmann are of the H-type, while the assumption of the preference for the rare by Ehrman, Probber, Watanabe, and Kawanishi is of the G-type. Their characteristics and implications can be tabulated as follows:

sociobiologists:	hierarchy	homogenization	fixed direction of evolution
Langlois and Roggman:	majority rule	homogenization	evolution halts
Ehrman, Probber, Watanabe, and Kawanishi:	situational	heterogenization	variable direction of evolution

Learning

(H) Sequential, and category-by-category. Teaching is transmission of information in a sequential order, usually verbal. Learn to classify and define. Abstract concepts are more important than specifics. The meaning is inherent in the definition and classification. Follow instructions step-by-step in learning how to do things.

(I) Isolate elements and understand the uniqueness of each.

(S) Learn by immersion into a situation and in a total context. Perceive and absorb all relations simultaneously. This is called "learning through the skin" by the Japanese. The new employees in large Japanese manufacturing firms are made to spend initial months or years in many parts of the firm ranging from assembly lines to retail shops, to learn by experience and by doing. Similarly, when foreign trainees arrive in Japan, they are often turned loose to experience and do whatever they wish, wherever, and in whichever sequence. Those who expect a sequenced, packaged, verbally explained training program often misinterpret this as a lack of willingness to teach.

(G) Japanese children are developing new extracurricular learning methods. There is evidence (Maruyama, 1985b) that children in Japan are learning not only faster but also qualitatively better from cartoonized educational books in sciences and history as well as from interactive videotape playback than from textbooks and classroom teaching. There are many series of cartoonized educational books published by several competing publishers. Children can use videotape players at commercial video centers that charge a few dollars for 30 minutes for the use of a machine but provide an unlimited number of tapes free. Many viewers accelerate the playback speed in order to save money, and can view in 30 minutes several tapes, each of which takes 60 to 90 minutes at the normal speed. More importantly, the viewer interacts with the machine in speeding up, slowing down, and rewinding the tapes, depending on the contents. This interactive viewing is very different from the passive viewing of television. From the point of view of the mathematical information theory, pictorial transmission to and storage in the brain have several advantages over verbal transmission (Maruyama, 1986a): (a) The amount of information that can be contained in one page of picture is much larger than that of one page of printed letters; (b) The brain can input all parts of a picture simultaneously, whereas verbal messages have to be inputted word by word. Consequently pictorial input is much faster than verbal input; (c) In a picture, the relations between parts can be seen as they are. If these relations have to be transmitted verbally, the picture has to be broken down into parts, and the relations among many parts have to be transmitted one by one. The receiving brain has to reconstruct the total network of relations. The process requires two epistemological conversions. Much information is lost in the conversion from picture to words, and distortions are inevitable in the reconstruction of the picture from the words. Consequently pictorial learning is more efficient than verbal learning. Data from rental stores show that Japanese children can read up to 20 cartoonized books a day, and view 7 or 8 video tapes in 30 minutes, retaining important details of the contents (Hakuhoodoo Trend Research Club, 1984). Two recent technological developments make it possible in the near future to replace verbal information and communication systems with picture-coded ones: (a) computer graphics, and (b) Chinese inventions of keyboard systems to compose pictorial elements *without* alphabetical or phonetical keyboard. Some might object that pictures cannot convey abstract concepts. However, it has been demonstrated that very abstract concepts can be accurately and compactly picture-coded (Maruyama, 1986a).

Trapped in One Mindscape Type

Not only business executives and managers but also eminent scholars can be trapped in a fixed mindscape type.

Ilya Prigogine's theory of nonequilibrium thermodynamics, which received a Nobel Prize in 1977, is mathematically of the G-type. However, he keeps falling back to H-type and I-type arguments. I have discussed the details elsewhere (Maruyama, 1980) that can be summarized: (a) Prigogine considers Democritus to be the forerunner and prototype of heterogenistic thinking who advocated an "atomistic" (individualistic) theory of the universe. (b) He stresses "dissipation" in arguing against traditional thermodynamics. There are two ways to break away from the 19th century thermodynamic theory based on random distribution of independent events. One is to consider causal loops instead of independent events. The other is to argue that the system has an energy input from outside. The two are logically independent of each other, even though most physicists including Prigogine assume that the second is required for the first. Mathematically, Prigogine does the first, but psychologically he falls back on the second. (c) What is important in a change-amplifying causal loop is *not* the initial kick, but the nature of the loop that amplifies a change steadily. But Prigogine puts more emphasis on fluctuations as an initial kick than on amplification. This tendency is of the H-type. (d) He uses the term *equilibrium* in the sense of decay into a random, homogeneous state instead of change-counteracting. This indicates his I-type tendency. (e) He is extremely interested in the process of bifurcation, particularly in connection with René Thom's catastrophe theory and its "singular points." Theorists of G-type mindscapes would consider any point in the process a potential branching point. But singular points have a lower density and cannot be everywhere. Prigogine looks at a singular point as a sort of prime mover. Furthermore, Thom's theory is based on nonloop causality. (f) Prigogine has shown a noticeable interest in the big bang theory, indicating his psychological need to find the prime mover.

The second example is the design of photoklystron arrays to transmit energy from an outer space station to the earth. At a conference at Princeton University in May 1979, the inventor Prof. John Freeman of Rice University presented his design in which the klystrons in the array were to be separately triggered with phase shifts. Upon hearing his lecture, the first thing that occurred to me was the effect of mutual induction among klystrons, which escaped his attention. After the lecture I asked him about it. His response was to *shield* each klystron against mutual induction. This surprised me, because mutual induction can be used as a self-tuning device for synchronization, wavelength control, and beam-direction control, to aim the beam perpendicular to the array surface. The Freeman design was to use the beam angle of 45°, which required time-phase shift. A design making use of mutual induction is much simpler, and saves the high cost of lifting the shield materials from the surface of the earth against gravity. I suggested that he consider using mutual induction. I thought his mindscape limitation strange, and asked the same question of what to do with mutual induction to two other eminent physicists independently, who were present at the conference: G. K. O'Neill of Princeton, and Henry Kolm of the Massachusetts Institute of Technology. They both said they would shield each klystron. Freeman went home and recalculated, and when the conference proceedings were published, he used the design using mutual induction. The important point is that psychologically he wanted to shield the klystrons, and only by mathematical calculation could he be convinced of the advantage of using the mutual induction. The mindscape limitation is more restricting than the intellectual ability.

Psychology and Mindscape Theory

The schemata theory in cognitive psychology has some relation to the mindscape theory. The schemata can be considered as subroutines of the mental process, whereas the mindscape provides overall principles for the schemata. Other branches of psychology, such as personality theory, industrial psychology, etc., are also relevant.

But in all cases, many psychologists would be interested in examining (a) the extent to which the mindscape types are innate or learned; (b) if learned, whether they can be unlearned or changed at a later stage in life; and (c) what would happen in the communication between different mindscape types.

Studies on the first question have been scarce. In fact, no study has directly addressed itself to this question. However, there is a study from which we can indirectly infer some answers: it is the controversial cerebral hemispheric functional interference study by Tsunoda (1978). I have discussed it in detail elsewhere (Maruyama, 1980). He conducted eight types of ingenious complex experiments meticulously, and his raw data are very solid, though difficult to replicate. But controversies and criticisms exist regarding his interpretation of the data. The eight types of his experiments are delayed auditory feedback interference; sound-type loading; delayed loading interference; frequency-modulated sounds and band-noise combinations; injection of chemicals into hemispheres; olfactory loading, and alcohol and tranquilizer loading; unilateral olfactory loading; and additional tests on congenitally blind subjects.

Let us take the first as an example. The subjects performed electrical key-tapping tasks much like the old telegrapher. Prior to the testing, the subjects practiced tapping of simple patterns such as three dots until they could repeat the patterns indefinitely without much effort. In the tests, auditory feedback reached one ear without delay and the other with a 0.2 second delay. Each tap activated a feedback of various types of tape-recorded sounds for 50 to 75 milliseconds. This short duration was chosen to prevent the subjects from identifying the nature of the sound. What the subjects heard were clicking sounds. The delayed-channel sound amplitude was gradually increased from the preadjusted level to the level that disturbed the tapping task. Then the channels were exchanged between two ears and the procedure was repeated.

The sensitivity difference between two ears had been pretested and the amplifier levels had been preadjusted. The difference between the disturbance threshold levels was interpreted to indicate which cerebral hemisphere was primary for that particular type of sound: the more sensitive to the interference, the more primary the hemisphere for that type of sound.

Tsunoda found that in the brains of the subjects who had been brought up in the Japanese way, including foreigners, "natural sounds" such as insect cries, bird songs, sounds of waves on a beach, and winds in a forest had primacy in the dominant hemisphere. On the other hand in subjects who had been brought up in North America and South America, including Japanese, the "natural sounds" had primacy in the nondominant hemisphere. From this, one may infer that the tendency is learned rather than innate. If mindscape types have anything to do with the tendency of treating natural sounds as verbal messages or as nonverbal emotional messages, then we might make a tenuous inference that such an aspect of mindscapes is learned rather than innate. Tsunoda's experiments used auditory stimuli. But responses to pictorial stimuli are much more discriminating in terms of mindscape types. If visual experiments can be devised at the level of sophistication comparable to Tsunoda's auditory experiments, they would be useful in examining whether some aspects of mindscape types are innate or learned. My objection to Tsunoda's theory is that he completely ignored the pictorial and spatial cognition, and generalized his conclusion from auditory experiments. Therefore, he concluded erroneously that the Japanese used the dominant hemisphere too much, and left the nondominant hemisphere underutilized.

On the second question as to whether one can change mindscapes later in life, there has been no direct experiment. One may, however, draw some indirect answers from Tsunoda's and Harvey's data. Among Tsunoda's subjects, there were some who had moved from one culture to another. In these very few subjects he found that moving after the age of 10 made the change of cerebral pattern difficult. But my hunch is that the age limit of irreversibility varies from individual to individual. Harvey's data, which is not longitudinal, showed that the percentage of System 1 (my H-type) is smaller in higher academic years among liberal arts majors, but a reverse tendency was found among education majors. Since the data are not longitudinal, he does not know whether the change is due to attrition or learning. Harvey's test cannot be administered to children because its stimuli are verbal statements that are difficult for children.

As for the communication between different mindscape types, I have discussed the problems in two articles (Maruyama, 1979a, 1985a). There are many types of distortions that occur. Dimension reduction may produce an internally consistent explanation and consequently a delusion of perfect understanding. Autodox is conversion of a counterargument into a proof of one's own theory. Further, a person's autodox may enable the opponents to argue that his autodox can be expected by their theories and therefore theirs are correct. But psychologically most damaging is unawareness of misunderstandings on both sides, which later leads to feelings of having been deceived, betrayed, or insulted. For example, the same statement "small is beautiful" may be supported by four mindscape types on different unstated grounds. H-type mindscapes can support it on the reasoning that since the entire region is homogeneous, nothing is lost by dividing it into smaller units. The I-type can reason that since all parts are different, it makes sense to let them be isolated. The S-type and G-type can support it because they see heterogeneity in the region, but on an unstated assumption that the different parts interact for mutual benefit. In my work in urban and regional planning, I found it useful to sort out different mindscape types behind a seeming agreement, in order to avoid later resentments and hostilities resulting from the delusion of agreement. In other cases, seeming disagreements disappeared when both sides became aware of mindscape differences.

Mindscape Subsedure

We have seen that in each culture, all individual mindscape types can be found, but some of them become dominant while others are superseded. This has three theoretical implications. (a) This view differs from the widely held notion that most of the persons in one culture are basically similar in their way of thinking and behaving, and that those who are dissimilar are abnormal or deviant. (b) The debate as to whether individual differences are smaller or greater than cultural differences is now seen in a new light. (c) Neonates are epistemologically heterogeneous.

There are several levels of transformation of nondominant types: (a) *Channeling*: Nondominant types are channeled to various professional or occupational niches. For example, during periods when H-type dominated, such as the eras of Descartes, Kant, Gothic buildings, etc., individuals with other mindscape types channeled their activities into fields such as painting, where their types were accepted and respected. (b) *Masking*: Individuals with nondominant types may disguise their types and practice them in a camouflaged form. (c) *Subsedure*: Some persons become capable of functioning in two patterns: their own type in a private life, and in the mainstream pattern in public or official life. Persons in subsedure are biscapal. (d) *Suppression*: The nondominant types may become unconscious or latent in individuals, either by external pressures such as acculturation, socialization, ostracism, marginalization, or indoctrination, or by internal processes such as repression, sublimation, internalization, or identification, but they can still be reactivated under favorable conditions. (e) *Loss*: If the suppression goes a step further, the individual may become incapable of reactivating his/her own pattern. There may be an age limit beyond which the transformation becomes irreversible. The age limit may vary from individual to individual. Subsedure is the opposite of supersedure, and is a conscious process.

Theoretical reformulations in several fields become necessary. In social sciences, research can be shifted from "culturally different ways of thinking" to "culturally different processes of transformation of nondominant types." In psychology, biscapalism can be studied as a healthy process and a higher ability than uniscapality, not as identity diffusion or schizoid pathology. The psychological environment of a society cannot be measured as healthy or unhealthy for all persons. It is a matter of good match or mismatch between the mainstream type and various individual types (Maruyama, 1959, 1961b). Ways to reactivate types that have become latent or unconscious, and to prevent irreversible transformation must be explored and devised.

Understanding across different mindscape types is impossible or very limited without biscapal translators. Even within a culture, interpersonal communication is often difficult for this reason. Biscapal persons acquire an important social role. Existing theories tend to assume that communication problems can be solved by giving more information, and puts an emphasis on methods of information transmission. This approach is outdated in cross-cultural and cross-scapal communication. Instead, we need to discover, identify, and mobilize biscapal persons. For example, in multicultural management, firms should not select foreign employees on the basis of the similarity of mindscape types between the former and the latter. "Foreigners who think like us" are not necessarily biscapal; they may be cultural deviants, exoconformists, or counterconformists. Exoconformists are those who conform to foreigners. There are also nonconformists who form a group and adhere to the group pattern. These are counterconformists.

Suppose that in culture A the mainstream type is X, and in culture B the mainstream type is Y. Other types Z, W, U, V . . . are nonmainstream types in both. A biscapal person in types R and S in culture T is denoted as RS/T. Then YX/A or XY/B can serve as direct cultural translator. There can also be indirect cultural translation via two persons, as follows: ZX/A and ZY/B can link together and translate between A and B through Z.

Difficulty of Communication and Management Across Mindscape Types

Understanding between different mindscape types is often very difficult or impossible, even when both parties are highly intelligent and willing. This is because each tries to interpret others in the framework of his/her mindscape and unwittingly distorts their meaning. As long as the distorted interpretation is *internally consistent*, the person is convinced that it is the correct interpretation. Types of distortion that occur frequently (Maruyama, 1961a, 1962, 1963b, 1979a, 1985a) are dimension reduction, self-proof, and autodox. Dimension reduction occurs when one reduces others' concepts into something within the dimensions available in his/her mindscape. Self-proof is construction of an interpretation that is internally consistent within his/her mindscape but incorrect and distorting from the others' point of view. Autodox is conversion of others' disagreements into a proof of one's own interpretation, often accompanied by self-proof. Illustrations, figures, and examples are given in the articles referenced above, especially that of 1985a. These distortions cannot be eliminated by transmission of more information, because the additional information gets distorted in the same way, reinforcing the misinterpretation rather than eliminating it. When one is unaware of the existence of mindscapes other than his/her own, one tends to think that the others are unintelligent, illogical, insincere, or deceptive (Maruyama, 1963b).

Use of Biscapal Persons as Transcapers

Policies and methods to discover and make use of biscapal persons are not yet developed and practiced in multicultural management situations where frictions abound. On the contrary, firms often make mistakes of employing and elevating cultural deviants whose mindscape types resemble those of the foreign superiors. For example, Indonesia has many ethnic groups. Japanese managers often make a mistake of elevating Bataks, whose characteristics resemble those of the Japanese, but who are different from and disliked by others.

Biscapal persons can be used as mindscape translators (abbreviated as "transcapers"). It is important to note that mindscape type translation (transcapation) is different from language translation and does not have to involve different languages. For example, between two mindscape types within the same country using the same language, transcapation may be needed.

There are two types of transcapers, (a) direct transcapers, and (b) indirect transcapers, as follows: Suppose that in country X, the dominant "mainstream" mindscape type is A, and other types B, C, D, E are under subsedure. On the other hand in country Y, type B is dominant and other types are under subsedure, as follows:

X: *Ax*, Bx, Cx, Dx, Ex.
Y: Ay, *By*, Cy, Dy, Ey

In this case Bx as well as Ay can serve as direct transcapers because each of them can understand the mainstream type of both countries. In the absence of direct transcapers, Cx and Cy can pair together and act as indirect transcapers because Cx understands C and A, and Cy understands C and B. Transcapation between A and B can be accomplished through the pair Cx-Cy. The same can be accomplished through other pairs such as Dx-Dy and Ex-Ey. However, C, D, and E are under subsedure in both countries and persons with these types must be discovered and identified.

Causal Relations Among Different Aspects of Behavior and Thinking

We are now able to see the interrelations among several seemingly unrelated aspects of our life such as science, politics, aesthetics, business management, and economics. We saw that different aspects of our behavior and thinking are related to mindscape types. "Behavior and thinking" is an awkward expression resulting from the H-type classificational epistemology. Instead of it, we may say "cogitact." Actually, behavior and thinking interact and shape each other, and are inseparable (Sartre, 1943). But can we say that the differences in mindscape types are the "cause" of the different patterns of cogitact? Such a way of asking a question is itself trapped in an H-type mindscape. Actually the patterns of cogitact influence the *learned* aspects of mindscapes. How about the *innate* aspects of the mindscape? Obviously they influence cogitact. But is the reverse also true? Consider the following. In all species with bisexual reproduction including humans, cogitact influences mate selection which in turn affects the genetic make-up of the offspring. In Homo sapiens, the criteria of mate selection depend largely on cultural and social considerations. In this sense cogitact influences the innate aspects of mindscapes.

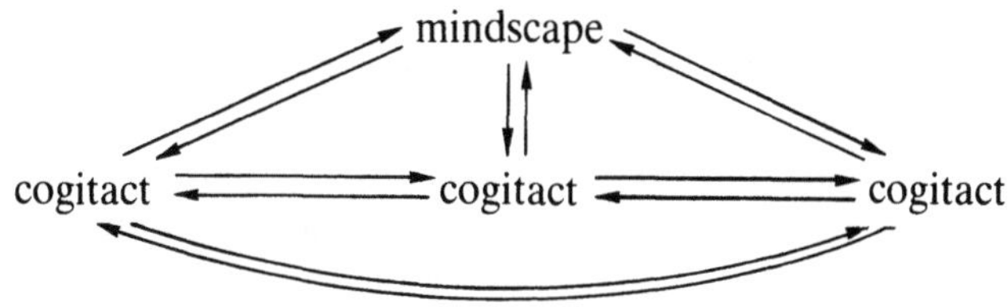

FIGURE 1.

Topics For Future Research on Mindscape Types

The research on mindscape types is still in its infancy. Here are some topics for research in the immediate future: (a) Which aspects of mindscape types are innate and which are learned? (b) The distinction between species-innate and individual-innate, and the latter's subdivision into hereditary-innate and nonhereditary-innate (for example, color-blindness is individual-innate and hereditary-innate whereas some dysfunction due to an accident during the fetal stage is nonhereditary-innate). (c) Which of the learned aspects are reversible, i.e., unlearnable? (d) Does the age limit and extent of reversibility vary from individual to individual? (e) The role of social pressures such as acculturation, socialization, marginalization, and ostracism. (f) The role of self-pressures such as repression, sublimation, identification, internalization, alienation, and attrition. (g) The role of mate selection, where the selection criteria can be both the cause and the effect of mindscape types.

To answer these questions, we need several types of studies: (a) longitudinal studies (to study the same individual at various ages), (b) effects of cross-cultural migration in childhood, (c) effects of cross-cultural migration in adulthood, (d) study of variations among siblings, and (e) study of biological relatives. For all these, we need psychological tests. Nonverbal tests are useful in multicultural studies and in studying children, to be correlated with verbal tests when testing adults. Development of these tests is at a very beginning stage (Maruyama, 1989c).

Conclusion

In this chapter, we have taken many concrete examples from international business management and economics, because they are some of the most complex problems requiring contextual understanding and solution. However, equally complicated problems exist in fields such as international environmental policy, large-scale outer space community design (Maruyama, 1976, 1984b) and crew selection (Maruyama, 1990b), and several other fields. The real problem, however, is not their complexity but our inadequate traditional intellectual structure. The problems are not "out there," but in our brain. We need G-type mindscapes instead of the established H-type mindscapes. We need epistemological reorientation and reorganization before any further economic or technological restructuring. The following chapters will elaborate on this point further.

References

Adorno, T. W., & Sanford, N. (1950). *Authoritarian personality*. New York: Harper.

Camara, S. (1975). The concept of heterogeneity among the Mandenka. *Technological Forecasting and Social Change*, *7*, 273–284.

Ehrman, L. (1972). Rare male advantages and sexual isolation in Drosophila Immigrans. *Behavior Genetics*, *2*, 79–83.

Ehrman, L. and J. Probber. 1978. Rare Drosophila males. *American Scientist* *66*:216–222.

Feuer, L. S. (1959). The bearing of psychoanalysis upon philosophy. *Philosophy and Phenomenological Research*, *19*, 323–340.

Gregory, G. (1986). *Japanese electronics technology: Enterprise and innovation*. New York: Wiley.

Hakuhoodoo Trend Research Club. (1984). *The fifth generation people*. Kyoto: PHP Research Institute.

Harvey, O. J. (1966). *Experience, structure and adaptability*. New York: Springer.

Kihlstrom, J. F. (1987). The cognitive unconscious, *Science*, *237*, 1445–1452.

Kluckhohn, C. (1949). The philosophy of Navajo Indians. In F. S. C. Northrop (Ed.), *Ideological differences and world order*. New Haven: Yale University Press.

Kubie, L. S. (1956). Some unsolved problems of the scientific career. *American Scientist*, *41*, 3–32.

Kuhn, T. (1962). *The structure of scientific revolutions*. Chicago: University of Chicago Press.

Langlois & Roggmann (1990). Comments. *Science 248*, 306.

Mannheim, K. (1929). *Ideologie und utopie*. Frankfurt: Schulte-Bulmke.

Maruyama, M. (1959). A critique of some widely held assumptions on the relationship between culture and menthal health (in French). *Revue de Psychologie des Peuples*, *14*, 273–276.

Maruyama, M. (1960). Morphogenesis and morphostasis. *Methods*, *12*, 251–296.

Maruyama, M. (1961a). Communicational epistemology. *British Journal for the Philosophy of Science 11*, 319–327; *12*, 52–62, 117–131.

Maruyama, M. (1961b). The multilateral mutual causal relationships among the modes of communication, sociometric pattern and intellectual orientation in the danish culture. *Phylon*, 22, 41–58.

Maruyama, M. (1962). Awareness and unawareness of misunderstandings. *Methodos*, *13*, 51–52, 255–275.

Maruyama, M. (1963). The second cybernetics: Deviation-amplifying mutual causal processes. *American Scientist*, *51*, 164–179, 250–256.

Maruyama, M. (1963b). Basic elements in misunderstandings. *Dialectica* (Switzerland) *17*(1), 78–92; (2–3), 99–110.

Maruyama, M. (1965). Metaorganization of information: Information in classificational universe, relational universe and relevantial universe. *Cybernetica*, *8*, 224–236.

Maruyama, M. (1972). Non-classificational information and non-informational communication. *Dialectica*, *26*, 51–59.

Maruyama, M. (1973). Human futuristics and urban planning. *Journal of American Institute of Planners*, *39*, 346–357.

Maruyama, M. (1974a). Paradigmatology and its applications. *Cybernetica*, *17*, 136–156, 237–281.

Maruyama, M. (1974b). Hierarchists, individualists and mutualists. *Futures*, *6*, 103–113.

Maruyama, M. (1976). Designing a space community. *Futurist*, *10*, 273–281.

Maruyama, M. (1977). Heterogenistics: An epistemological restructuring of biological and social sciences. *Acta Biotheoretica*, *26*, 120–136.

Maruyama, M. (1978a). Heterogenisics and morphogenetics: Toward a new concept of the scientific. *Theory and Society*. *5*, 75–96.

Maruyama, M. (1978b). Endogenous research and polyocular anthropology. In R. Holloman & S. Arutiunov (Eds.), *Perspectives on ethnicity, series world anthropology*. Den Haag: Mouton.

Maruyama, M. (1979a). Trans-epistemological understanding. In R. Hinshaw (Ed.), Currents in anthropology (Sol Tax festschrift). Den Haag: Mouton.

Maruyama, M. (1979b). Mindscapes. *World Future Society Bulletin*, *13*, 13–23.

Maruyama, M. (1980). Mindscapes and science theories. *Current Anthropology*, *21*, 589–599.

Maruyama, M. (1981). Denkmuster: Meta-prinzipien der Umweltgestaltung. *Garten und Landschaft*, October, 806–815.

Maruyama, M. (1982). Four different causal metatypes in biological and social sciences. In W. Schieve & P. Allen (Eds.), *Self-organization and dissipative structures*. Austin: University of Texas Press.

Maruyama, M. (1984a). Alternative concepts of management: Insights from Asia and Africa. *Asia Pacific Journal of Management*, *1*, 100–111.

Maruyama, M. (1984b). Aesthetics and environment in outer space, subterranean and underwater communities. *Futures*, *16*, 148–162.

Maruyama, M. (1985a). Mindscapes: How to understand specific situations in multicultural management. *Asia Pacific Journal of Management*, *2*, 125–149.

Maruyama, M. (1985b). The new logic of Japan's young generations. *Technological Forecasting and Social Change*, *28*, 351–364.

Maruyama, M. (1985c). Experience looping, design looping and concept crossing. *Futures*, *17*, 385–389.

Maruyama, M. (1986a). Toward picture-coded information systems. *Futures*, *18*, 450–452.

Maruyama, M. (1986b). Morphogenetic economics: Change-amplification by causal loops. *Technological Forecasting and Social Change*, *29*, 205–213.

Maruyama, M. (1987a). Japan's agricultural policy failure. *Food Policy*, *12*, 123–126.

Maruyama, M. (1987b). New economic thinking: Morphogenetic causal loops and product adaptation strategy. *Futures*, *19*, 437–441.

Maruyama, M. (1989a). Epistemological sources of new business problems in the international environment. *Human Systems Management*, *8*, 71–80.

Maruyama, M. (1989b). Cultural models of international borrowing. *Human Systems Management*, *8*, 213–216.

Maruyama, M. (1989c). Practical steps for interactive inventions. *Technology Analysis and Strategic Management*, *1*, 423–430.

Maruyama, M. (1990a). Some realistic considerations in the economic reorganization of East European countries. *Academy of Management Executive*, *4*, 90–91.

Maruyama, M. (1990b). Organizational structure, training and selection of outer space crew members. *Technological Forecasting and Social Change*, *37*, 203–212.

Maruyama, M. (1990c, June). International proactive marketing. *Marketing Research*, 36–49.

Mead, M. (1937). *Cooperation and competition among primitive peoples.* New York: McGraw-Hill.

Minsky, M. (1975). A framework for representing knowledge. In P. H. Winston (Ed.), *The psychology of computer vision.* New York: McGraw-Hill.

Myrdal, G. (1944). *The American dilemma.* New York: Harper & Row.

Myrdal, G. (1957). *Economic theory and underdeveloped regions.* London: Duckworth.

Rokeach, M. (1960). *Open and closed minds.* New York: Basic Books.

Sartre, J.-P. (1943). *L'Être et le Néant.* Paris: Gallimard.

Shannon, C. and Weaver, W. 1949. *Mathematical theory of communication.* Urbana: University of Illinois Press.

Tsunoda, T. (1978). *Nipponjin no noo.* Tokyo: Taishuukan.

Uchihashi, K. (1982). *Takumi no jidai.* Tokyo: Koodansha.

Ulam, S. (1960). Lecture given at Stanford University.

Watanabe, T. and Kawanishi, M. 1979. Mating preference and the direction of evolution in Drosophila. *Science*, *205*, 906–907.

Watsuji, T. (1935). *Fuudo.* Tokyo: Iwanami Shoten.

2
Hyperinflation, Culture, and Morphogenetic Economics in Argentina

ENRIQUE G. HERRSCHER, ROBERTO M. HERRSCHER, and MARCELO DIAMAND

In a previous paper (Herrscher, 1986), one of the authors of this chapter used the expression "should be countries" or SBC, to designate countries that by most environmental standards should be developed, but are not.

In these cases, *the isolation of many parts of the social system prevents development, whereas that same nondevelopment stands in the path of efforts to remedy the lack of coalescence of the different elements of society.*

Maruyama (1963) has provided a framework for the study of loops of this kind. In a first phase, human mental processes started with simple, unidirectional cause-effect relations. In a second phase (Maruyama's "first cybernetics") certain feedback processes were described, by which the effect influences the cause, until the system's equilibrium is again reached. In a third phase, we recognized that our preference for self-correcting ("deviation-counteracting") feedback networks was highly biased, and that we had neglected the cases of *deviation-amplifying mutual causal systems*, where the feedback does not close the gap of disequilibrium, but widens it. This third phase is what Maruyama denominates "second cybernetics."

So-called less developed countries (LDCs), and particularly SBCs, are a fertile ground to apply these "second cybernetics." In this chapter we will use Maruyama's theoretical framework in our contextual analysis to relate cultural, social, political, geographic, and historical factors to the problem of stagnation, hyperinflation, and economic crisis in

---

Reprinted with permission from E. G. Herrscher, R. M. Herrscher, "Systemic Aspects of Hyperinflation in Argentina," *Human Systems Management*, 9(1990)2, pp. 89–105.

Argentina. Argentine economist Diamand's (1973, 1978, 1986, 1988) economic model will be used, and a systems approach will be applied.

Based on van Gigch's hierarchy of inquiring systems (van Gigch, 1986; van Gigch & Pipino, 1986), we could visualize the following levels and their corresponding models:

1. The user's level, producing a descriptive model of the world.
2. The observer's level, producing an explanatory model.
3. The designer's level, producing a prescriptive model.
4. The epistemologist's level, producing a paradigmatic model.

On the basis of that classification, we could say that the present chapter follows a theme track that started with several contributions to recent annual meetings of the International Society for Systems Sciences (ISSS):

A 1986 ISSS paper (Herrscher, 1986) analyzed such loops mainly from the user's level, providing a *descriptive* model (and to a lesser degree an explanatory one).

A 1987 ISSS paper (Herrscher, 1987) and 1988 articles (Herrscher, 1988a, 1988b) referred to those loops from the observer's level, providing mostly an *explanatory* model (and to a lesser degree a prescriptive one).

A 1989 ISSS paper (Herrscher et al., 1989) addressed these issues from a designer's level, providing mostly a *prescriptive* model.

The present chapter, starting from an explanatory and prescriptive approach, and using some issues of the above papers, tries to reach the epistemologist's level, providing a first attempt toward a *paradigmatic* model.

The reason for selecting Argentina as a case study is that its inability to solve its paralysis and extricate itself from 40 years of inflation—turned hyperinflation in 1989/1990—point to a systemic problem.

Argentina used to be rich, but not developed. What is the difference between these two labels? In a way, it is similar to the difference between development and growth. For a system, such as a nation, to "develop," it is not sufficient for one or very few elements of the system to "grow." A significant portion of major elements of the system must grow as well, harmoniously and simultaneously, enhancing one another synergically. In other words, we define "development" as "equilibrated growth."

Argentina's wealth and spectacular growth in the five decades from 1880 through 1930 was due to its exports of agricultural commodities, mainly beef, corn, and wheat. During the following five decades, the traditional European meat market disappeared, and so did most of the grain market.

What happens in a country that is deprived of its major source of income while it does not find another? *Rich-country structures are no longer viable. Rich-country expectations can no longer be fulfilled. Mismanagement, formerly invisible because of one single sector's efficiency, can no longer be overlooked. And violent struggle for income arises.*

Decadence leads to the appearance of numerous vicious circles—deviation-amplifying loops of mutual causality—that become very difficult to break. Thus, Argentina can be considered a paradigmatic case study for the emergence and maintenance of a "*system of vicious circle systems*" (Herrscher, 1988b).

Our focus here is not the precise factual description, but the *conceptual implications* of an actual case. Hence, no quantitative data will be presented. Our purpose is to highlight the intricate web of relations of cultural features, sociological characteristics, and economic variables that make it so difficult for a relatively advanced society to make full use of its resources and solve its paralyzing problems. In this context, given the "ease" Argentine inflation becomes hyperinflation, both will be treated as one continuing phenomenon.

This case study is not applicable to traditionally poor countries. For them, scarcity of human, physical, and technological resources is an objective stumbling block. However, once such scarcity is overcome, ideological and organizational obstacles take its place.

In this case, past splendor ceases to be an asset, and becomes a liability. The gap between what *was* and what *is* creates a sense of forfeited rights, a high level of expectations, and country-wide idle capacity, with not enough immediate opportunities to foot the national economic bill.

Many of these problems are of cultural and sociological nature, and originated long before the above-mentioned splendor disappeared. The next section will deal with these problems. They will constitute the framework for the economic analysis and comments of the following two sections. The final section will present certain conclusions from a systemic and cybernetic viewpoint.

The notation system of the diagrams, taken in part from Maruyama (1986), is as follows:

1. If A affects B directly, we put an arrow from A to B.
2. If an increase in A causes an increase in B, and a decrease in A causes a decrease in B, then the arrow carries a plus sign.

3. If an increase in A causes a decrease in B, and a decrease in A causes an increase in B, then the arrow carries a minus sign.
4. If A has "soft" influence in B, that is, the historical origin of B can be tentatively traced to A, without a continuing effect such as in items 2 or 3 above, we put a dotted line arrow from A to B. Note that all influences in the sociocultural section are "soft," whereas most of the ones in the economic section are "hard" (full lines). Note also that dotted line arrows have no plus or minus signs.
5. (P) over an arrow from A to B indicates that A is not sufficient to cause B, but makes B possible.
6. References from one diagram to another, or references to uncoded concepts of the text, are indicated with balloons. Alternative theories per Figures 9 and 10 are excluded from this rule.
7. Capital letters indicate key words used in other sentences and in the diagrams.
8. Numbers in the diagrams refer to coded sentences in the text. In the section Sociocultural Characteristics, they correspond to synthetic features, and in the section Argentina's Morphogenetic Economics, to relations between variables.

For the sake of brevity, national characteristics are described *as if* they were absolute values (which of course they are not). Similarly, certain causal relationships are drawn *as if* they were simple and lineal. Needless to say, most propositions that follow are oversimplified, and correspond to a complex, relative, and often ambiguous reality.

Moreover, the diagrams do not show the all-important *time factor*. In social systems, a causality from A to B is rarely stable; it usually either increases or decreases. Often, A may even ceases, while B outlives A's disappearance and continues inertially on its own. In other words, we acknowledge the shortcomings of static diagrams to represent dynamic processes. In spite of this mechanistic simplification, we believe that our analysis may be useful for future research along these lines.

Sociocultural Characteristics

It is impossible to understand Argentine economy without reference to its historical, sociological, and cultural background. These aspects obviously constitute a unit. Their presentation in separate paragraphs, as well as the segregation of the present section from the economic one, are both arbitrary, only justified in terms of practicality. In fact, some economic aspects will appear in this section and some sociocultural aspects in the next.

Argentina, in the southern cone of South America, far away from the economic centers, is a SCARCELY POPULATED country, with 30 million people scattered in 3 million square kilometers. Long distances make integration difficult. Moreover, half of the population of Argentina lives in or near Buenos Aires (BA), its capital. CENTRALIZATION is such that all roads (literally and metaphorically) lead to BA.

1. Economic-Cultural Context

1.1. In the beginning, during the Spanish conquest (see 4.1), the major human stream was not constituted by pioneers. Military heroism and endurance, as well as individual GREED AND OPPORTUNISM, were the major motives.

1.2. Gold and silver, initially the main economic values, were not obtained by production nor industrialized further. They passed as WINDFALL GAIN through the economy; they promoted neither Latin America's development, nor Spain's.

1.3. Thus, the economic system was based on EXTRACTION, not manufacturing of goods.

1.4. Later, cattle and grain, due to the fertility of the pampas, reproduced the same model of an EXTRACTIVE ECONOMY, not a productive one.

1.5. Instead of a culture of effort, such easy availability of valuable goods originated a RENTISTIC CULTURE. By this term we mean the attitude of expecting wealth as a gift from heaven, as opposed to having to create wealth with effort.

1.6. Rentistic culture promotes HEDONISTIC VALUES based on easy life and luxury, and the expectation of continuing windfall gains.

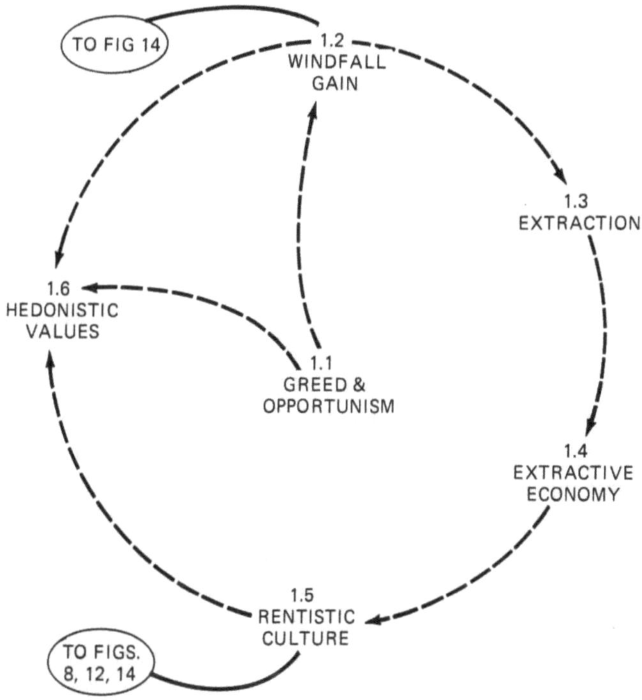

FIGURE 1. Economic-cultural context.

2. *Historical-Cultural Context*

2.1. DISPERSED NATIVES, who had never constituted empires like in Peru or Mexico, were conquered easily.

2.2. After Moors and Jews were expelled from Spain in the 15th Century, Spanish culture became ANTIPLURALISTIC.

2.3. COLONIAL ADMINISTRATION was centralized, i.e., all decisions were taken by Spain.

2.4. Culture of this territory was AUTHORITARIAN, inherited from Spanish "MACHISMO."

2.5. After independence in 1816, a SCHISM appeared, as two "countries" emerged: the HARBOR of BA, with a European culture, and the interior, with a "GAUCHO" culture (Luna, 1985).

2.6. Perception of reality became SCHIZOPHRENIC. Urban and rural population, BA and interior, immigrants and Spanish heritage, did not integrate easily. Faced with MASSIVE IMMIGRATION (see 3.2) the original "criollo" often was at once paranoid and smart, combining a DON QUIXOTE charging against imaginary enemies, with a SANCHO PANZA trying to profit from the situation.

2.7. The TANGO, "sadness that became a dance," showed these cultural clashes, and the resulting split perception of reality.

2.8. Lack of COMMON VALUES (see 7.4) promoted a very WEAK OBEDIENCE to the legal system: "*many laws, but no Law*" (Aguinis, 1988).

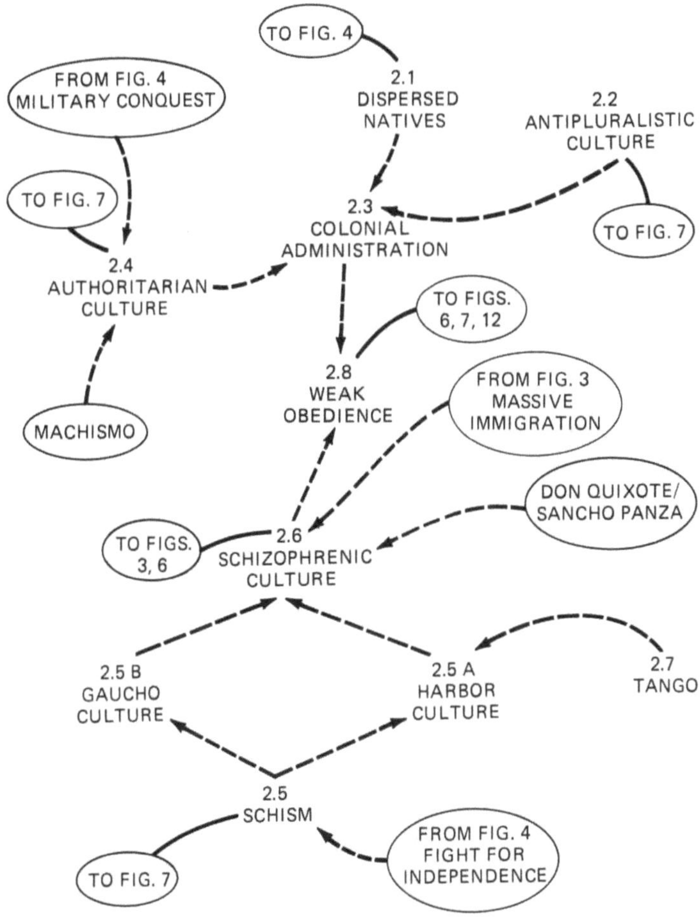

FIGURE 2. Historical-cultural context.

3. *Social Context*

3.1. CONCENTRATION: few people owning vast extensions of land.

3.2. MASSIVE IMMIGRATION: 6 million people between 1860 and 1930. By end of the century, over 30% of the population were immigrants (against 15% in the United States). Unlike Canada or Australia, these immigrants came from a great variety of countries, without a common home culture.

3.3. INDUSTRIALIZATION attracts people from rural to urban areas.

3.4. Immigrants have little or NO ACCESS TO THE LAND.

3.5. Immigrants OVERCROWD BA: by 1914 more than half of the population of BA was born abroad.

3.6. URBAN SATURATION: population grows more rapidly than the infrastructure.

3.7. SLUMS and shanty towns grow.

3.8. Population grows WITHOUT cultural and SOCIAL COHERENCE (Labourdette et al., 1989).

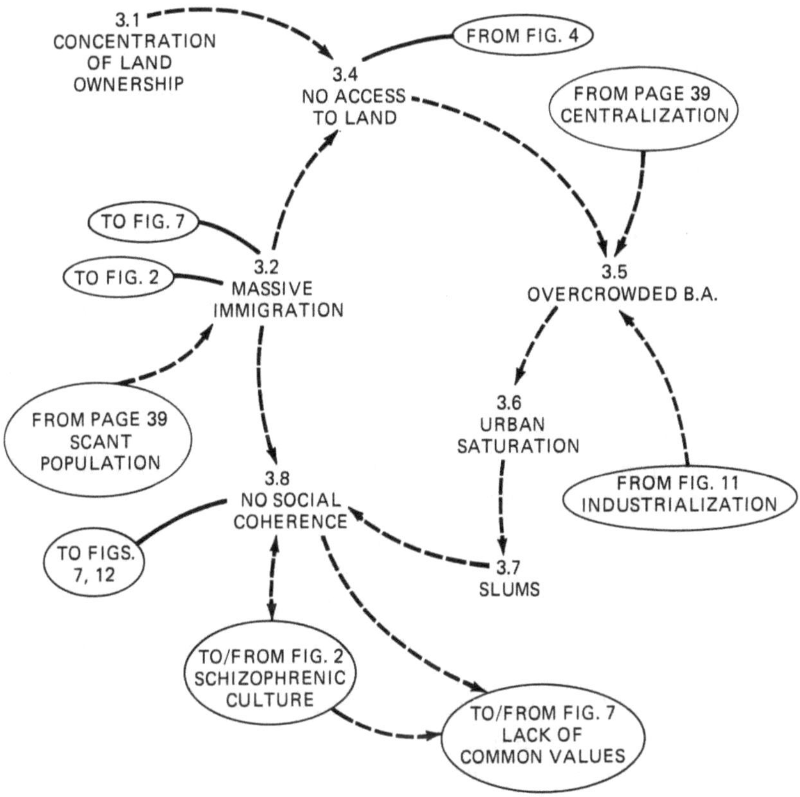

FIGURE 3. Social context.

4. Military Context

4.1. The territory was conquered by MILITARY CONQUEST, not "colonized" (except for isolated efforts by the Jesuit order).

4.2. The FIGHT FOR INDEPENDENCE (1810) started as a municipal revolt in BA, then spread to the rest of the territory by military action(Romero, 1956).

4.3. MILITARIZATION OF PATRIOTISM: "Only arms can defend the nation."

4.4. Most of the FERTILE LANDS were conquered militarily; much of it was given to officers, often in lieu of salary. Many traditional families started that way.

4.5. Hence (4.1 through 4.4), the HISTORICAL IMPORTANCE of the armed forces.

4.6. The armed forces see themseives as GUARANTORS OF NATIONAL IDENTITY.

4.7. The armed forces forge frequent ALLIANCES with the economic power and the Church, thus strengthening their role of guarantor.

4.8. In the 1970s, the insertion in the cold war—the so-called NATIONAL SECURITY DOCTRINE—further strengthened such a role.

4.9. POLITICAL INSTABILITY is both the cause and the result of that military "guarantee."

4.10. This led during long periods to a high degree of "MILITARIZATION OF POLITICS" (Kovadloff, 1987) and to frequent MILITARY INTERRUPTIONS to the democratic process.

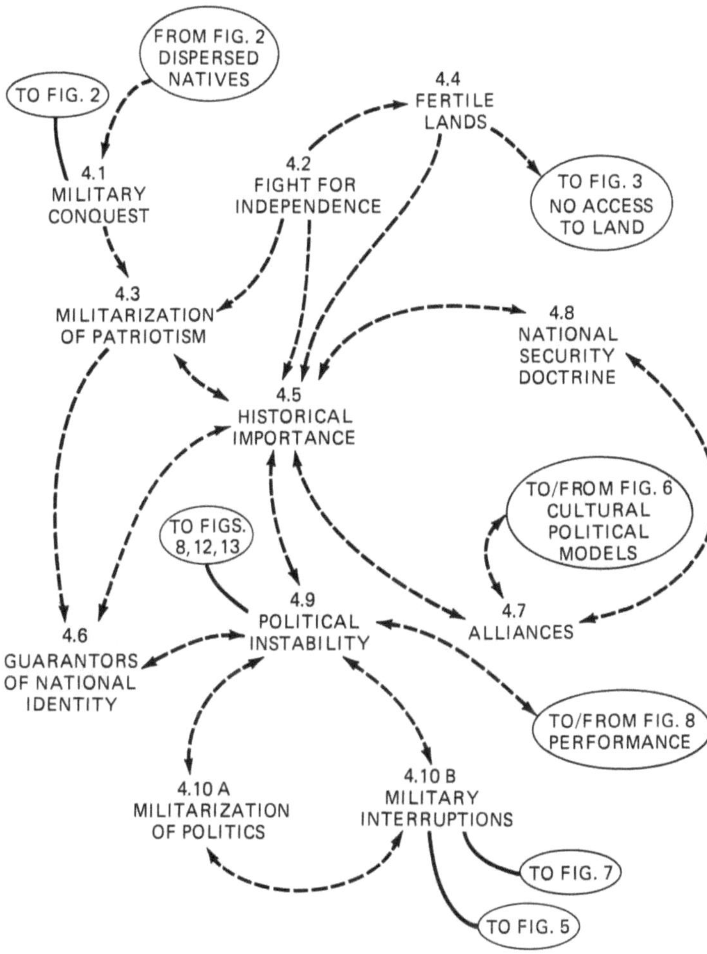

FIGURE 4. Military context.

5. *Political System Context*

5.1. Military interruptions caused change to proceed by "LIMITED REVOLUTIONS": 1812, 1820, 1852, 1891, 1930, 1943, 1955, 1962, 1966, 1976.
5.2. Economic POWER RELATIONS were not substantially changed by these political processes.
5.3. Such processes often lead to DICTATORSHIPS supported by traditional groups and economic powers.
5.4. Gradually, INTERNAL CONFLICT reappeared and political weakening of the system took place.
5.5. Democracy was then restored, but a RESTRICTED DEMOCRACY emerged, due to guarantees granted to military and economic pwers.
5.6. SOCIAL AND POLITICAL CHALLENGES to the economic powers appeared gradually.
5.7. FREEDOM OF EXPRESSION developed, as these challenges increased.
5.8. DEMOCRACY'S DILEMMA emerges: either challenge leads to SOCIAL CHANGE, or challenge is SUPPRESSED.
5.9. Suppression of challenge is achieved either by a formal democracy with growing RESTRICTIONS or by a new DICTATORSHIP.

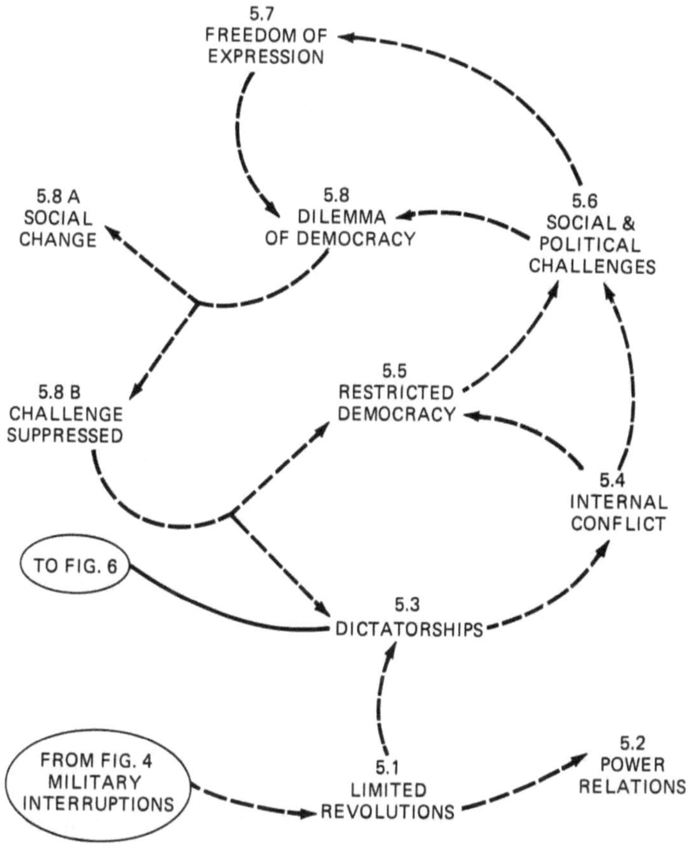

FIGURE 5. Political system context.

6. *Foreign and Local Influence Context*

6.1. As soon as independence was declared, the Argentine territory became a sort of BRITISH HINTERLAND, where wool and other raw materials required by industry were extracted more cheaply than in Europe.

6.2. At a time when in the United States the industrializing North prevailed over the commodities-exporting South, Argentina took the opposite road: the fertile coast (the central pampa and the BA harbor) imposed FREE TRADE over the timidly industrializing interior.

6.3. The result was DELAYED INDUSTRIALIZATION: infantile industries thus lacked the initial kick of temporary protection that would have allowed early development.

6.4. A CULTURAL-POLITICAL MODEL emerged, based on European (mostly British) influence.

6.5. Key of the model was the ANGLO-ARGENTINE ALLIANCE, comprising a closely knit rural and trade elite.

6.6. Mostly BRITISH INVESTMENTS (railways, electricity, telecommunications, etc.) provided the infrastructure for the massive transatlantic trade, enhancing at the same time the initial steps of internal development.

6.7. Culturally, the influence was mostly French: the CULTURAL CENTER VALUES imposed fashion, music, later film, and overall modes of perception.

6.8. BA imposed its already COLONIZED IDEALS on the interior.

6.9. World Wars I and II, by stopping most imported supplies, provoked a FORCED INDUSTRIALIZATION, mainly oriented toward consumption.

6.10. As from World War I and even more World War II, both economic and cultural power shifted to the United States, enhancing (as from the 1950s, mostly via television) imported consumption VALUES: "be like the United States."

6.11. World War I: the first wave of industrialization facilitated the ascent of a large MIDDLE CLASS that strove for power, mainly first and second generation immigrants.

6.12. In 1916 the ruling elite finally accepted true democratic elections, and thus the RADICAL PARTY came to power.

6.13. Between the wars, industrialization advanced mainly by foreign impulse, through subsidiaries of MULTINATIONALS.

6.14. World War II: the second wave of industrialization attracted MASSES OF WORKERS from the provinces and formed the basis of Peron's labor support.

6.15. In 1943 to 1946, the new social configuration, plus the example of European fascism, paved the way of PERONISM to power.

6.16. The UNIONS, consolidated under Peron with strong mutual support, acquired political strength and independence after Peron's fall in 1955.

6.17. PUBLIC ADMINISTRATION, important since Spanish times, acquired increased strength under Peron's centralized state, and grew even more with the military regimes that followed, as well as with Radical Party administrations.

6.18. Growth of public administration caused continuing PUBLIC INEFFICIENCY and FISCAL DEFICIT.

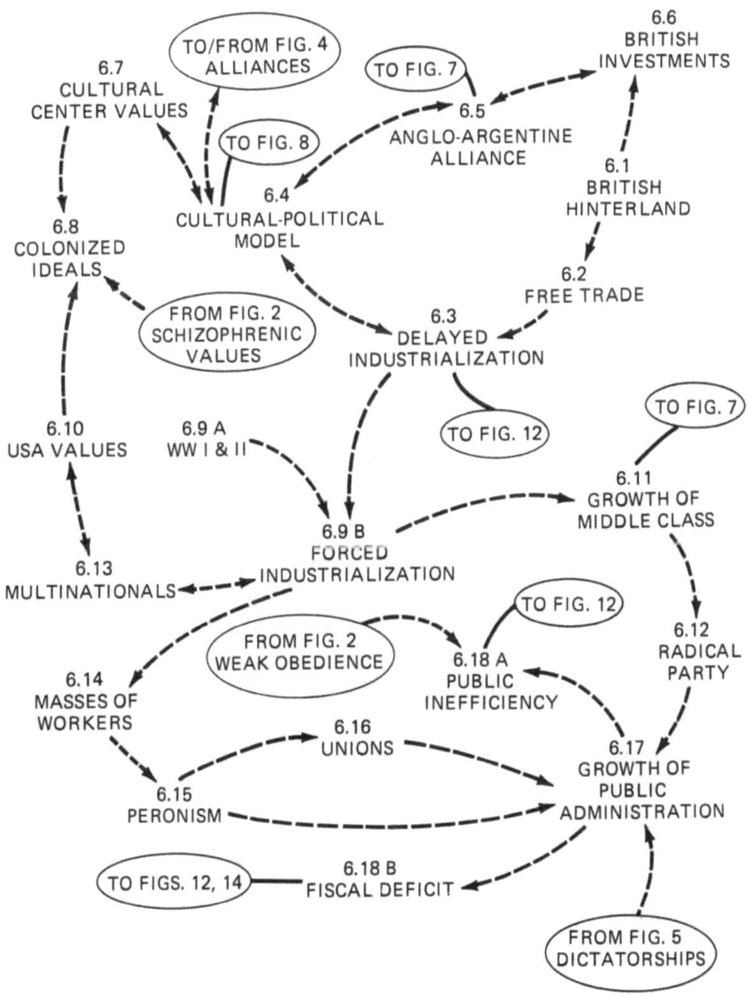

FIGURE 6. Foreign and local influence context.

7. *Psychosociological Context*

7.1. Spanish military conquest of the Indian territory brought with it a high level of INTOLERANCE.

7.2. The 1810 quest for independence did not represent a unified political process: the SCHISM between the rich pampa with its harbor and all the other provinces caused long periods of civil wars, and was never healed (Romero, 1956).

7.3. The Anglo-Argentine alliance of the late 19th century created the modern Argentina, but was bound to be elitist and thus was based on a FRAUDULENT POLITICAL SYSTEM.

7.4. Massive diversified immigration from Europe, massive flight from rural to urban areas, and spontaneous immigration from neighboring countries did not produce a social coalescence, but a LACK OF COMMON VALUES.

7.5. Such lack of common values facilitated the frequent MILITARY INTERRUPTIONS to democratic law.

7.6. Military interruptions DELAYED the democratic LEARNING PROCESS. With little or no democratic learning process, common values did not develop.

7.7. Military interruptions also weakened the sense of responsibility: officials of civilian governments did not face reelection but possibly a coup d'état; officials of military governments were not held accountable by civilian institutions; thus, a society with NO REWARD/PUNISHMENT SYSTEM developed.

7.8. The CHURCH, always near power in a mainly Catholic country, tried to provide common moral values, but often did not break the barrier of hypocrisy, and traditionally leaned strongly toward the Status quo, including the military regimes.

7.9. The middle class, oppressed between an unreachable elite and an emerging working class, exercised little participation once its representatives reached power: PASSIVITY resulted.

7.10. Passivity of most constituents separated the leaders from the people, and facilitated NONETHICAL BEHAVIOR (bribes, privileges, etc.).

7.11. During military regimes, excessive authority of armed forces and civilian TECHNOCRATS provoked further passivity of the population.

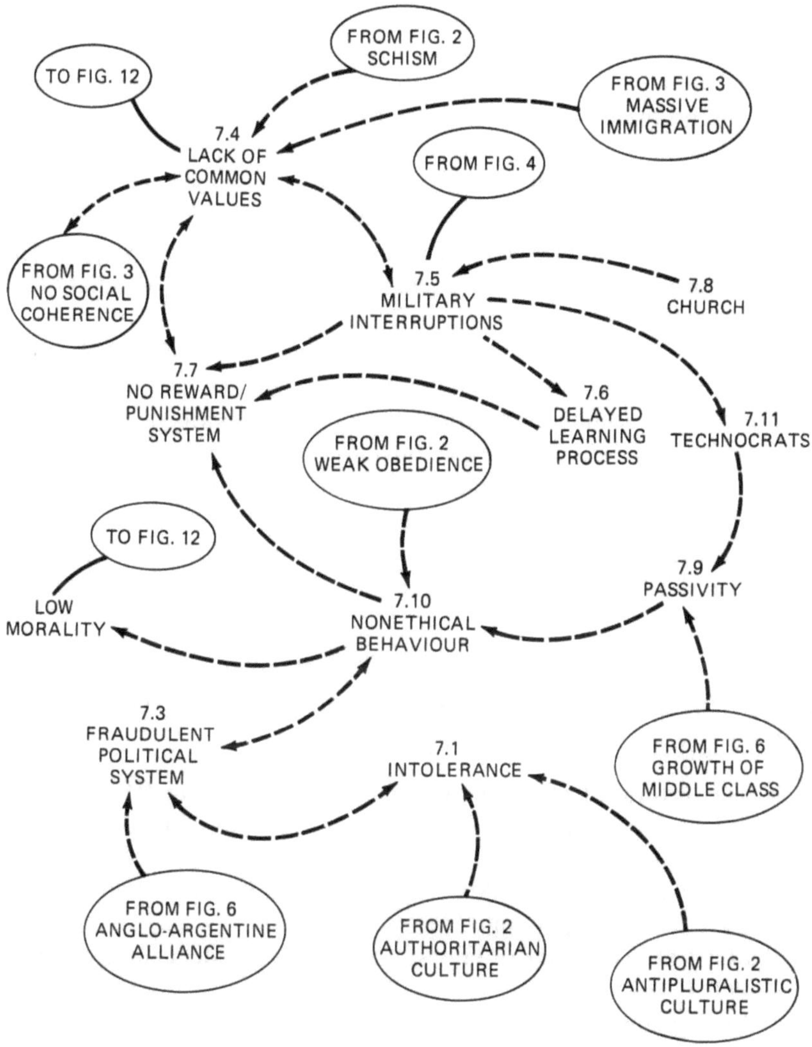

FIGURE 7. Psychosociological context.

Argentina's Morphogenetic Economics

In a country that is self-sufficient in food and almost self-sufficient in energy, the main problem resides in shortcomings of organization and policy. With these two terms, we refer to human constructs that define how decisions are made, value relations are established, and transactions are effected. History and cybernetics play an important role here. Social organization has developed through myriads of adaptative processes, some deviation-counteracting, most deviation-amplifying causal loops (Maruyama, 1986). The foreign debt problem adds an additional vicious circle to the situation.

In this section, we will try to present very synthetically the most important causal circuits that describe the Argentine economy. As in the preceding section, the different loops are described and drawn separately only for convenience: obviously, all loops are interrelated and form in reality a complex network that intermingles with the sociocultural aspects of the preceding section.

Some explanations that expand the very synthetic links between variables will follow in the next section.

8. *Theoretical Model Loop* (see The Issue of the Theoretical Model on page 70 and The Issue of Full or Idle Capacity on page 71)

8.1. The historical background of a RENTISTIC CULTURE, plus the influence of FOREIGN CULTURAL PARADIGMS, lead to the use of an INADEQUATE theoretical economic MODEL.

8.2. An INADEQUATE MODEL causes SOCIAL MISUNDERSTANDING of economic reality.

8.3. SOCIAL MISUNDERSTANDING causes inadequate economic POLICIES.

8.4. Inadequate POLICIES cause unsatisfactory economic PERFORMANCE.

8.5. Unsatisfactory PERFORMANCE causes POLITICAL INSTABILITY of the democratic system (social support of democracy will have low priority if basic needs are not satisfied).

8.6. In turn, POLITICAL INSTABILITY causes unsatisfactory PERFORMANCE (how can you plan if you do not know what political system will exist tomorrow).

8.7. POLITICAL INSTABILITY plus unsatisfactory PERFORMANCE increase influence of INADEQUATE MODEL (when things go astray in one's country, one tends to follow the policies of countries that are already fully developed).

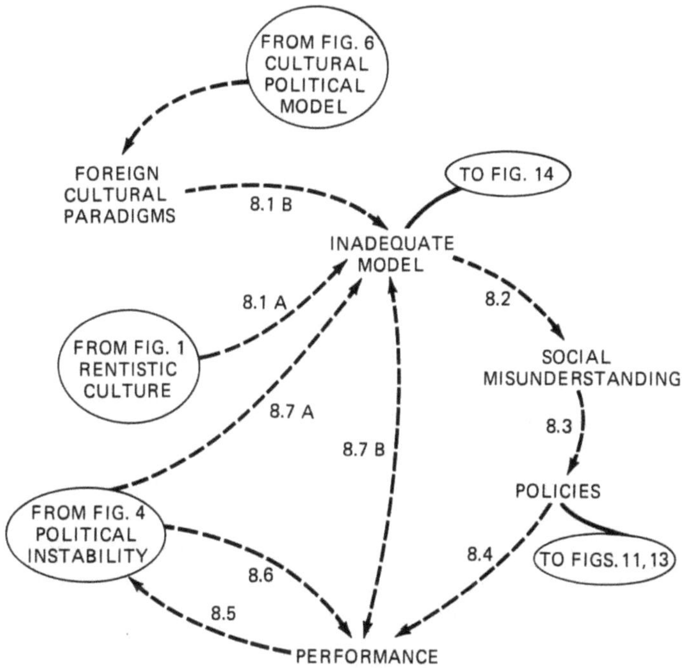

FIGURE 8. Theoretical model loop.

9. *Orthodox (Neoclassic) loop* (Alternative assumption I: full capacity—see The Issue of Full or Idle Capacity on page 71)

9.1. Insufficient prior SAVINGS cause inadequate productive INVESTMENTS.
9.2. The MARKET MECHANISM assures that the economy is working at FULL CAPACITY.
9.3. Thus, only additional INVESTMENTS or increase of efficiency can cause growth of SUPPLY.
9.4. Industrial INEFFICIENCY decreases supply.
9.5. Industrial INEFFICIENCY increases the need for INDUSTRIAL PROTECTIONISM.
9.6. In turn, INDUSTRIAL PROTECTIONISM allows and favors industrial INEFFICIENCY (if protection is perceived as permanent, many industries will rely on protectionism instead of pursuing efficiency).
9.7. Excessive size of the state (produced by GROWTH OF PUBLIC ADMINISTRATION), vis-à-vis its limited ability to collect taxes, causes FISCAL DEFICIT.
9.8. FISCAL DEFICIT causes increase of MONEY SUPPLY.
9.9. Increase of MONEY SUPPLY causes increase of DEMAND.
9.10. *Given the key assumption of full capacity*, the increased DEMAND leads to "demand in excess of productive capacity," and thus to INFLATION.
9.11. INFLATION decreases SAVINGS in local currency (it is not worthwhile to save in a weak currency).
9.12. INFLATION increases FISCAL DEFICIT (the Olivera-Tanzi effect: expenditures are cash, whereas tax collections, due to time lag, are diluted by inflation).
9.13. INFLATION increases INEFFICIENCY (by lack of a stable currency, corporate planning and control are rendered difficult).

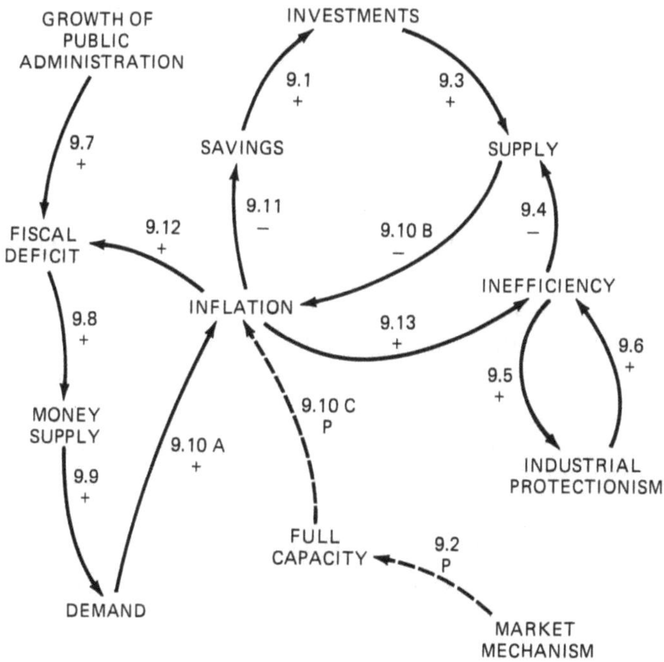

FIGURE 9. Orthodox (neoclassic) loop.

10. Populist (Keynesian) Loop (Alternative assumption II: idle capacity—see The Issue of Full or Idle Capacity on page 71)

10.1. The MARKET MECHANISM *does not assure by itself the full utilization of capacity.* Even if it reaches equilibrium, this may be obtained below that level, and IDLE CAPACITY results.
10.2. Existing IDLE CAPACITY makes it possible for the SUPPLY to grow.
10.3. FISCAL DEFICIT increases MONEY SUPPLY.
10.4. MONEY SUPPLY increases DEMAND.
10.5. Increased DEMAND, GIVEN EXISTING IDLE CAPACITY, causes an actual increase of SUPPLY.
10.6. Increase of SUPPLY causes (is equivalent to) growth of ECONOMIC ACTIVITY (as measured by grass national product [GNP]).
10.7. Growing ECONOMIC ACTIVITY stimulates INVESTMENTS.
10.8. New INVESTMENTS increase (IDLE) CAPACITY.

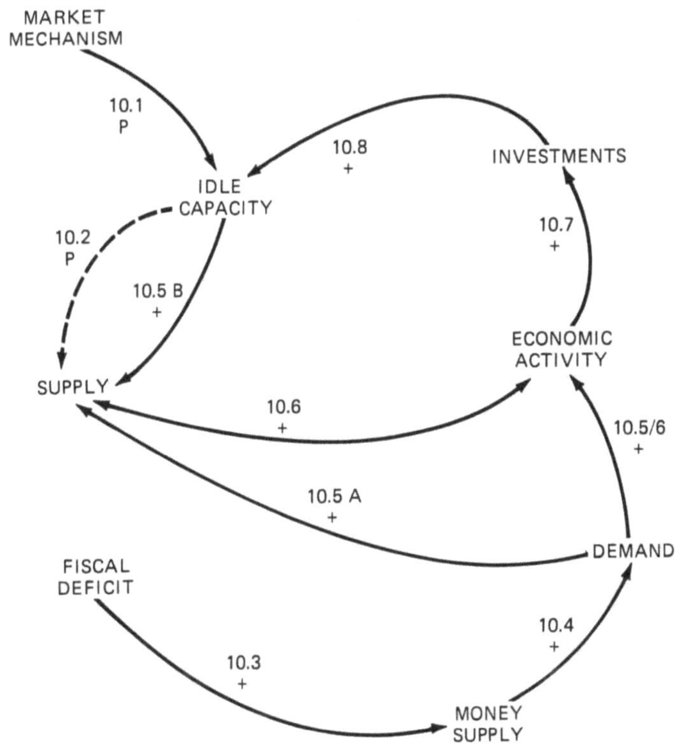

FIGURE 10. Populist (Keynesian) loop.

11. Foreign Exchange Loop (see The Issue of Foreign Exchange Shortage on page 72)

11.1. High productivity of NATURAL RESOURCES, initially almost sole export, cause INADEQUACY OF EXCHANGE RATE: it will be adequate for said privileged commodities, but *too low for everything else* (industry, services, and natural resources less favored by nature).

11.2. INADEQUACY OF EXCHANGE RATE, combined with INEFFICIENCY (see next loop), cause lack of international competitiveness of industrial products: NONCOMPETITIVENESS (according to classical theory, the exchange rate should offset inefficiency, but 11.1 prevents this effect from happening).

11.3. NONCOMPETITIVENESS causes lack or slow growth of INDustrial EXPORTS (INDEXPORTS).

11.4. Process of INDUSTRIALIZATION needs capital goods and imported materials, and therefore requires foreign exchange: DOLLAR REOUIREMENTS.

11.5. DOLLAR REQUIREMENTS, combined with stagnant INDEXPORTS, cause a foreign exchange GAP: *industrialization needs more foreign funds than it produces.*

11.6. FOREIGN PROTECTIONISM, combined with law of DECREASING agricultural RETURNS and with FOREIGN, more advanced TECHNOLOGY, limits the growth of AGRIcultural EXPORTS (AGRIEXPORTS).

11.7. The process of industrialization decreases the "substitution scope" (number of areas where additional substitution is worthwhile). Thus, as INDUSTRIALIZATION advances, the import SUBSTITUTION process has a declining productivity.

11.8. GAP, combined with said limitations of INDEXPORTS, AGRIEXPORTS, and SUBSTITUTION, cause chronic SHORTAGE OF FOREIGN EXCHANGE.

11.9. SHORTAGE OF FOREIGN EXCHANGE provokes economic POLICIES designed to restore balance of payment equilibrium.

11.10. Economic POLICIES call for MONETARY RESTRICTIONS and, generally, MAXIDEVALUATIONS (see 13.13).

11.11. MAXIDEVALUATIONS transfer income from low saving and high consuming sectors, to high saving and low consuming sectors (INCOME TRANSFER).

11.12. INCOME TRANSFER reduces DEMAND.

11.13. MONETARY RESTRICTIONS reduce DEMAND.

11.14. Reduced DEMAND induces RECESSION.

11.15. RECESSION causes LOWER PRODUCTION.

11.16. As an alternative to induced recession, SHORTAGE OF FOREIGN EXCHANGE will cause lack of critical inputs required for production: BOTTLENECKS will originate.
11.17. BOTTLENECKS cause LOWER PRODUCTION.
11.18. LOWER PRODUCTION produces IDLE CAPACITY.
11.19. LOWER PRODUCTION reduces BOTTLENECKS.
11.20. LOWER PRODUCTION, either caused by recession or by bottlenecks, reduces SHORTAGE OF FOREIGN EXCHANGE.

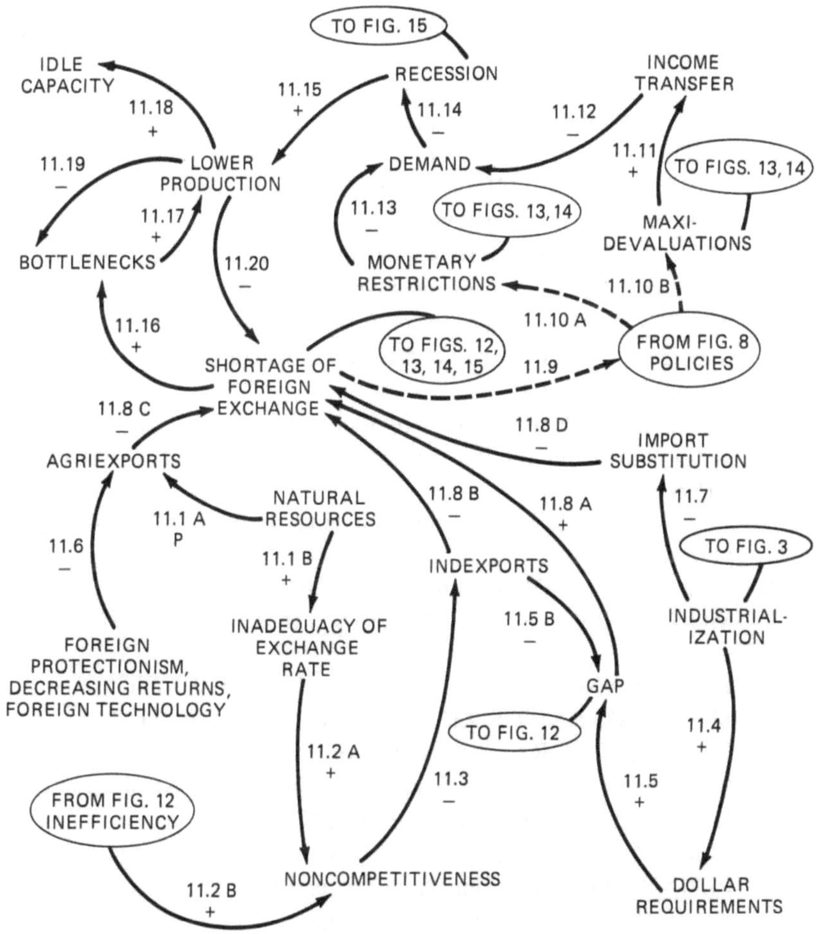

FIGURE 11. Foreign exchange loop.

12. *Efficiency Loop* (see The Issue of Inefficiency on page 74)

12.1. Historical background of a RENTISTIC CULTURE, combined with POLITICAL INSTABILITY, cause UNDERDEVELOPMENT, due to lack of suitable conditions for harmonious growth.
12.2. UNDERDEVELOPMENT causes context-dependent industrial INEFFICIENCY. (Inefficiency is defined as higher cost or lower output than comparable activities elsewhere.)
12.3. UNDERDEVELOPMENT causes a weak INFRASTRUCTURE.
12.4. Weak INFRASTRUCTURE increases INEFFICIENCY.
12.5. UNDERDEVELOPMENT causes a weak TECHNOLOGY base.
12.6. Weak TECHNOLOGY increases INEFFICIENCY.
12.7. UNDERDEVELOPMENT, combined with RENTISTIC CULTURE and POLITICAL INSTABILITY, produce a LOW MORALITY of the system.
12.8. LOW MORALITY increases private INEFFICIENCY. (Morality is defined as the proportion of nonrational, nonpositive benefit-cost–based decisions over total number of decisions, due to bribes or other illegal actions in the private, and especially in the public, sector.)
12.9. PUBLIC INEFFICIENCY (evidenced by high cost and bad performance of public services) increases private INEFFICIENCY.
12.10. FISCAL DEFICIT absorbs and thus reduces SAVINGS in private hands.
12.11. Reduction of SAVINGS increases FINANCIAL COSTS.
12.12. MONETARY RESTRICTIONS increase FINANCIAL COSTS.
12.13. High FINANCIAL COSTS increase INEFFICIENCY.
12.14. SMALL MARKET SIZE reduces economy of SCALE.
12.15. Low INDEXPORTS reduce economy of SCALE.
12.16. Small economy of SCALE increases INEFFICIENCY.
12.17. IDLE CAPACITY increases INEFFICIENCY.
12.18. POLITICAL (and economic) INSTABILITY causes POOR PLANNING (when regulations change daily, the planning horizon tends to be extremely short range).
12.19. POOR PLANNING causes POOR MANAGEMENT.
12.20. WEAK OBEDIENCE, DELAYED INDUSTRIALIZATION, NO SOCIAL COHERENCE, and LACK OF COMMON VALUES cause POOR MANAGEMENT.
12.21. POOR MANAGEMENT increases INEFFICIENCY (this

means that the above-indicated context-dependent inefficiencies do not exclude additional self-generated inefficiencies).

12.22. INEFFICIENCY, combined with INADEQUACY OF EXCHANGE RATE for industry (see 11.1) cause industrial NONCOMPETITIVENESS abroad.

12.23. NONCOMPETITIVENESS increases the INADEQUACY OF EXCHANGE RATE for industry.

12.24. NONCOMPETITIVENESS, *not inefficiency by itself*, increases the need for INDUSTRIAL PROTECTIONISM.

12.25. NONCOMPETITIVENESS prevents INDEXPORTS.

12.26. Absence of INDEXPORTS provokes foreign exchange GAP.

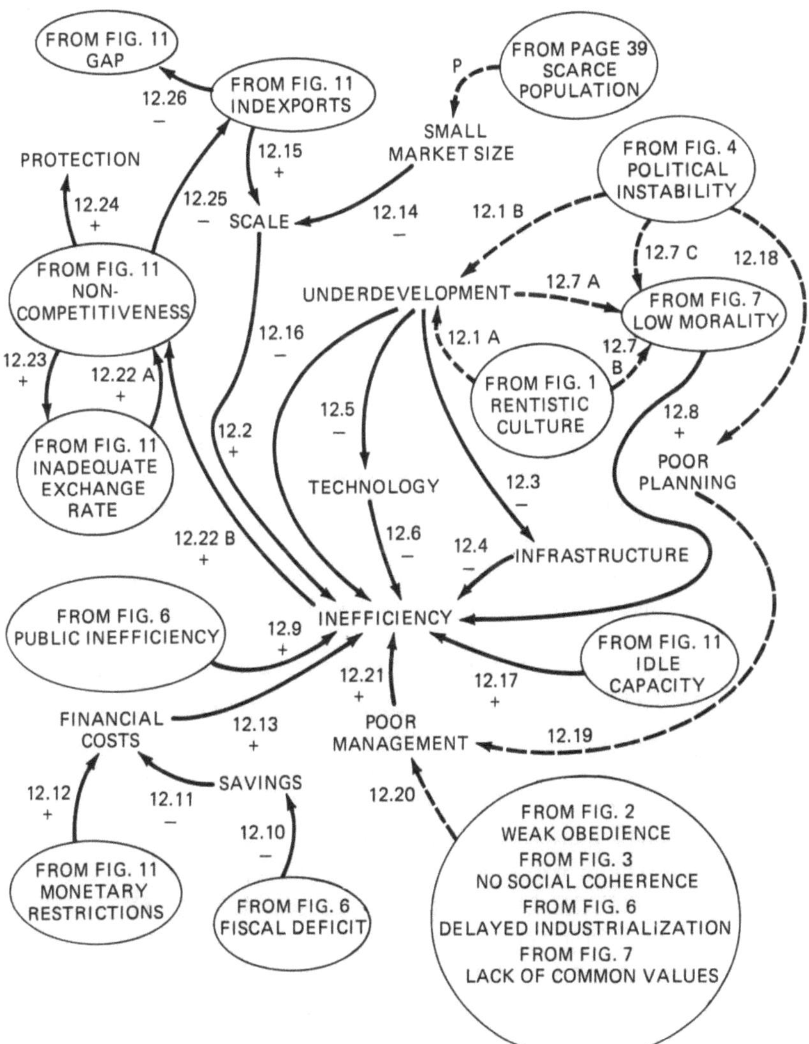

FIGURE 12. Efficiency loop.

13. Foreign Debt Loop

13.1. SHORTAGE OF FOREIGN EXCHANGE causes chronic need to incur in FOREIGN DEBT (mechanism follows).
13.2. SHORTAGE OF FOREIGN EXCHANGE causes NEED TO ATTRACT foreign capital.
13.3. NEED TO ATTRACT requires INCENTIVES.
13.4. INCENTIVES require high LOCAL INTEREST RATE.
13.5. At the same time, INCENTIVES require some DEVALUATION LAG, defined as a *temporary delay of the subsequent devaluation.* In other words, in order to "attract," a country must "first increase the exchange rate strongly, then leave it alone."
13.6. Petrodollars and volatile financial markets (FINANMARKETS) enhance AVAILABILITY of foreign credits.
13.7. INCENTIVES combined with AVAILABILITY cause increase of FOREIGN DEBT.
13.8. When a FOREIGN DEBT international CRISIS sets in, it will cause an increase of FOREIGN INTEREST RATES.
13.9. FOREIGN DEBT plus FOREIGN INTEREST RATES cause significant increase of interests due that, for the portion unable to be paid, accrues as COMPOUND interest.
13.10. COMPOUND interests cause further increase of FOREIGN DEBT.
13.11. FOREIGN DEBT, combined with SHORTAGE OF FOREIGN EXCHANGE, calls for support and intervention of the International Monetary Fund (IMF).
13.12. IMF demands economic POLICIES to restore balance of payments equilibrium.
13.13. Economic POLICIES call for reduction of demand through increased MONETARY RESTRICTIONS and MAXIDEVALUATION (see 11.10).
13.14. SHORTAGE OF FOREIGN EXCHANGE, combined with DEVALUATION LAG, cause PERCEPTION of imminent devlaution.
13.15. PERCEPTION CAUSES CAPITAL FLIGHT, both of local capital and of the foreign capital that came.
13.16. FLIGHT increases PERCEPTION.
13.17. FLIGHT provokes POLITICAL INSTABILITY.
13.18. POLITICAL INSTABILITY causes LACK OF CONFIDENCE in government.
13.19. LACK OF CONFIDENCE causes FLIGHT.
13.20. FLIGHT increases LOCAL INTEREST RATES.

13.21. PERCEPTION stops inflow of fresh capital (NONINFLOW).

13.22. FLIGHT, combined with NONINFLOW, increase the pressure and finally make the MAXIDEVALUATION inevitable.

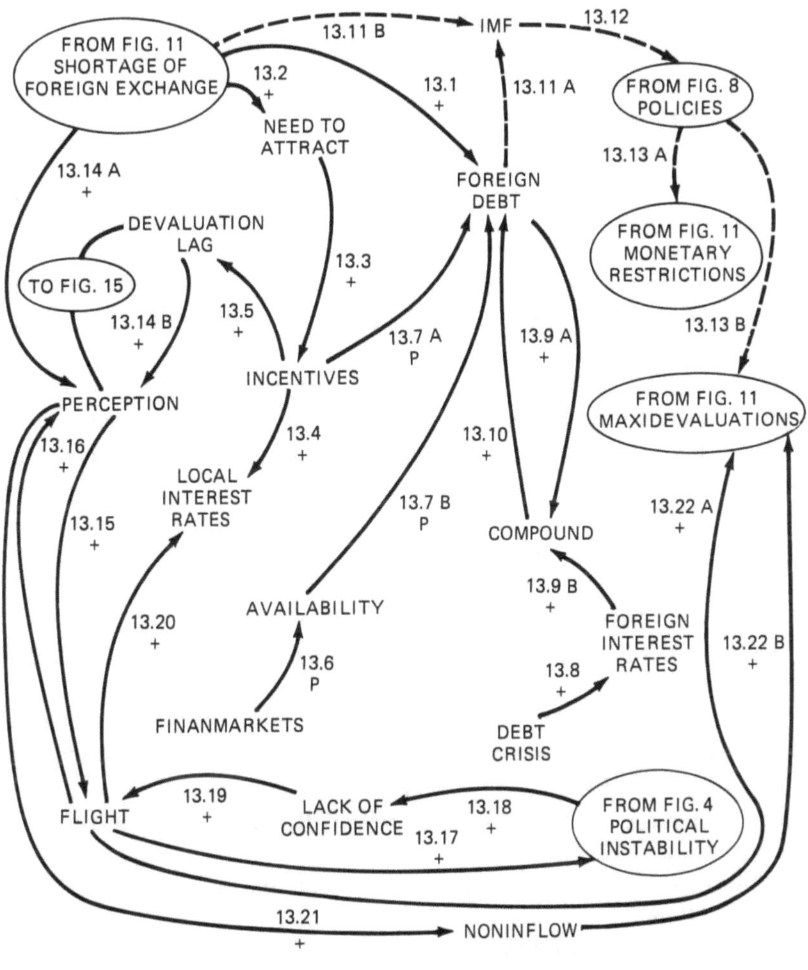

FIGURE 13. Foreign debt loop.

14. Inflation Loop (see The Issue of Inflation on page 75)

14.1. MAXIDEVALUATION causes local price increases of exportable and imported goods (TRANSPRICE INCREASES).
14.2. TRANSPRICE INCREASES produce INFLATION.
14.3. TRANSPRICE INCREASES cause significant RELATIVE PRICE VARIANCES. The INFLATIONary process itself makes this phenomenon possible, and enhances it.
14.4. RELATIVE PRICE VARIANCES cause drastic REDISTRIBUTION of income.
14.5. REDISTRIBUTION causes RESISTANCE to redistribution of income (no social sector is willing to relinquish economic power).
14.6. Historical background of former WINDFALL GAIN and of RENTISTIC CULTURE cause high consumption level EXPECTATIONS.
14.7. REDISTRIBUTION, combined with RESISTANCE and with EXPECTATIONS, cause violent STRUGGLE for income.
14.8. INFLATION produces loss of purchasing power, insecurity, and impossibility to save in local currency, all of which lead to STRUGGLE.
14.9. STRUGGLE causes cost-push INFLATION (see 14.19).
14.10. INFLATION combined with an INADEQUATE MODEL cause MONETARY RESTRICTIONS.
14.11. MONETARY RESTRICTIONS increase LOCAL INTEREST RATES.
14.12. The need to finance FISCAL DEFICIT, given the maintenance of monetary restrictions (see 15.4 alternative), increases LOCAL INTEREST RATES.
14.13. Increase of LOCAL INTEREST RATES increases FINANCIAL COSTS.
14.14. Increase of FINANCIAL COSTS increases cost-push INFLATION.
14.15. Increase of LOCAL INTEREST RATES, on the other hand, decreases the incentives to buy, to invest and to hold inventory, thus reducing DEMAND.
14.16. Reduction of DEMAND reduces ECONOMIC ACTIVITY as measured by GNP.
14.17. Reduction of ECONOMIC ACTIVITY, through weakening of the bargaining force of many participants, reduces STRUGGLE.
14.18. On the other hand, reduction of ECONOMIC ACTIVITY, by

depriving most sectors of much of their income and wealth, increases STRUGGLE.

14.19. Reduced STRUGGLE reduces the pressure toward INFLATION, whereas more violent STRUGGLE increases the pressure toward INFLATION (see 14.9).

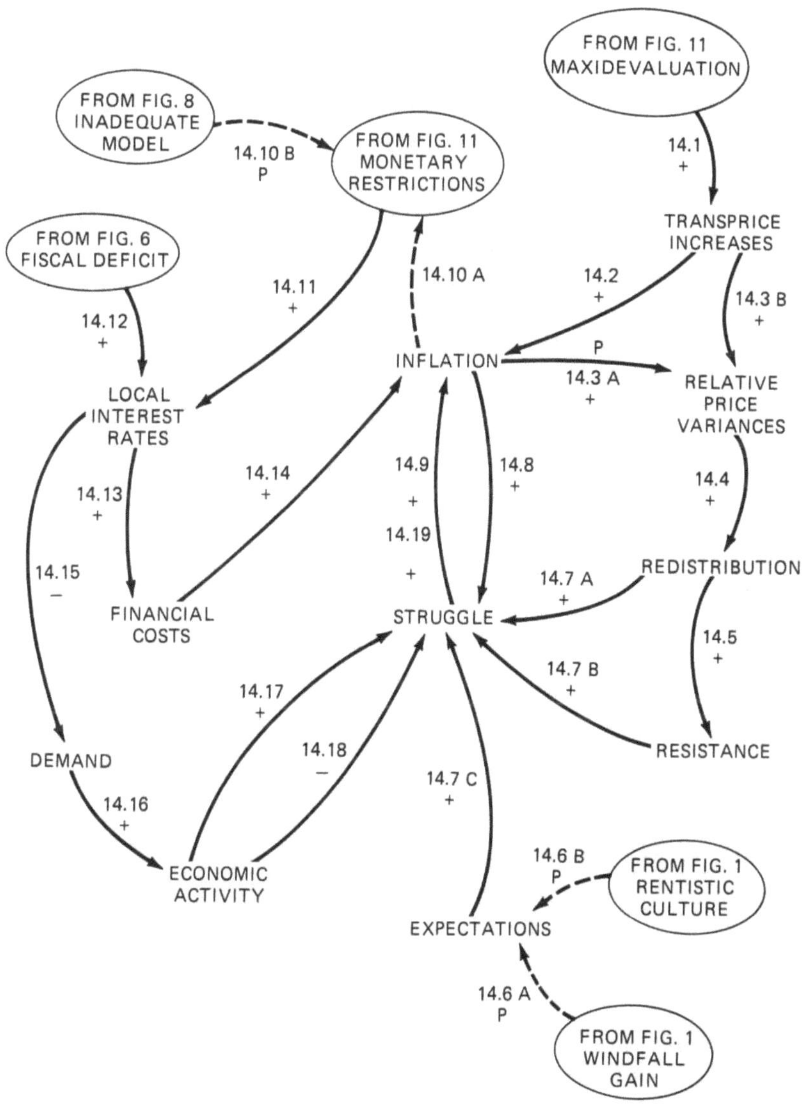

FIGURE 14. Inflation loop.

15. Reactivation Loop

15.1. DEVALUATION LAG (defined as delay of the occurrence of the next maxidevaluation) allows a temporary improvement of SALARIES.

15.2. Improvement of SALARIES increases DEMAND.

15.3. Induced RECESSION, in spite of its intent to the contrary, will increase FISCAL DEFICIT, because of lower taxation basis.

15.4. The need to finance FISCAL DEFICIT, given the maintenance of "normal" local interest rates (see 14.12 alternative), increases MONEY SUPPLY.

15.5. MONEY SUPPLY increases DEMAND.

15.6. If quicker than increase of SUPPLY, increase of DEMAND will lead to INFLATION.

15.7. If, on the other hand, SUPPLY keeps pace with DEMAND, ECONOMIC ACTIVITY will increase.

15.8. Increase of ECONOMIC ACTIVITY will cause increase of IMPORTS.

15.9. Increase of IMPORTS makes the SHORTAGE OF FOREIGN EXCHANGE reappear.

15.10. Reappearance of SHORTAGE OF FOREIGN EXCHANGE provokes PERCEPTION of further imminent maxidevaluations, and thus, the inflation–capital flight–foreign debt loops set in.

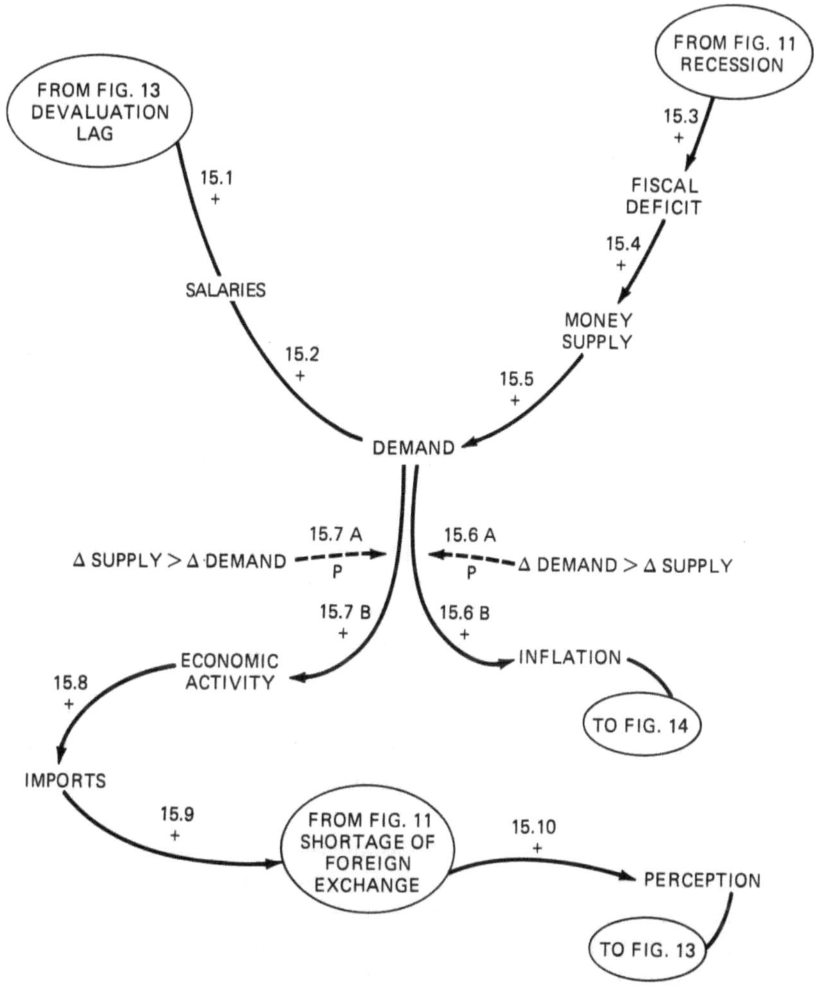

FIGURE 15. Reactivation loop.

Comments

A complete description of each of these variables and interrelations would exceed the scope of this chapter, However, some comments will help explain the complexities of the issues at hand, as well as sharpen the distinction between causal loops that correspond to morphogenetic economics applicable to any country, and causal loops that refer especially to developing countries, and specifically to the Argentine case.

The Issue of the Theoretical Model

Maruyama (1986) discusses the inadequacy of existing economic theories and models. In Argentina this inadequacy is particularly significant, for the following reasons:

1. Argentina has a traditional preference for imported goods and ideas. As the country grew rich without major effort, there was *no need* to develop a model that would apply specifically to Argentina. Economic theories were "imported" from abroad, particularly from England, where most goods, capital, and economic systems originated.
2. Two types of transactions exist in developing countries: those carried out in local currency, and those carried out in "internationally acceptable currency"—read, in foreign exchange. Traditional economic virtues, like hard work, efficiency, or sacrifice, will *not affect* foreign exchange except by way of higher exports or lower imports.
3. There is nothing wrong, in developing countries, with copying, duly adapted, the policies that more advanced countries implemented to *reach development.* However, policies to reach development are quite different from policies that apply only once the country *is developed.* For example, free trade is to be favored once you are economically powerful, but you need protection until you reach that position.
4. Free exchange market and open borders should assure the most efficient application of resources. However, what results in "unbalanced productive structures" (Diamand, 1973) i.e., in a country of two widely different levels of efficiency, is that the exchange rate is established at the level where the privileged natural resources, which can be extracted cheaply, can be exported. For all activities not so favored by nature, that level is insufficient. Thus, industry and all natural products other than the ones privileged by nature or protection, are *condemned to live only within the scope of the domestic market*, which generally is insufficient to support the growth of infantile or diversified activities.

5. This means that *nontraditional exports* must not only compete abroad; but first they must compete against the traditional, nature-favored activity that sets the exchange rate.
6. On the other hand, *traditional (agricultural) exports* are inelastic: they are solely ruled by foreign demand.
7. Growing countries need foreign exchange. Unless they *only* carry out their specialized trade, such as oil, coffee, or agriculture—in other words, unless they forget about development—they chronically run short of foreign exchange.
8. "Normal science" proposes, as the only remedy for chronic exchange shortages, a recession that diminishes imports. Thus, constant stop-go discontinuities that delay development occur.
9. What began as a blessing, ends up as a curse: due to an inadequate uniform exchange policy, based as much on the dictum of economic theory as on the danger of mismanagement of differential exchange rates, the harmonic development of the economy is inhibited—not by international competition, but because it is impossible to compete against the oil, copper, coffee, meat, or corn *of one's own country*.
10. Due to substitution of natural by artificial products, or due to other technological advances, or due to sheer protectionism of the developed countries, those privileged products tend now to lose their markets. When this occurs, *past neglect* of the rest of the possible activities leaves the country in disarray.
11. Technological research generally favors labor-saving capital investments. In highly developed countries, where capital is relatively cheap and labor relatively expensive, labor-saving technologies make sense. Those are precisely the countries where research is performed and technological advance is achieved. In countries where capital is relatively expensive and labor relatively cheap, those technologies may not apply (Geyer & van der Zouwen, 1982).
12. The "theoretical model loop" shows the resulting vicious circle: the application of an indequate model leads to a profound misunderstanding of economic reality by all levels of the population, particularly of the political leadership, which leads to inadequate economic measures. The resulting poor economic performance further strengthens the tendency to apply orthodox theories, the application of which caused the trouble in the first place.

The Issue of Full or Idle Capacity

As opposed to Keynesian economics, the monetarist theory is based on the premise that no idle capacity exists. This supports the monetarist explanation of inflation: an increase of money supply will increase demand, which will pull up prices. This may often be the case with "typical" developing countries, which emerge from poverty. However, it is not the case with what we call "should be countries" like Argentina. Its decline from a period of wealth assures the existence of ample idle capacity. This means that, in principle, Argentina is the perfect candidate for the application of Keynesian economics. However, three reasons render such "chronical idle capacity" dubious, and hence classical theory emerges once again:

1. Capacity very quickly becomes obsolete. *Obsolescence*, as well as *poor maintenance*, is one of Argentina's major problems.
2. Even if idle installed capacity exists, this alone does not warrant additional supply, once a "Keynesian money injection" takes place; the owners of the factories must be willing to increase production. It would seem obvious that every industry would jump to the possibility of reducing its idle capacity. However, in times of *economic and political instability*, this may not hold true. Hence the danger, in extreme turbulence, of additional funds fueling capital flight instead of feeding production.
3. The most important restriction to the notion of idle capacity in developing countries is the *availability of foreign exchange* (see next subsection).

The Issue of Foreign Exchange Shortage

The fact that, when the country runs out of dollars, idle capacity is useless, is the major restriction that renders the Keynesian model not applicable. In other words, it is *the shortage of foreign exchange what causes the constant stop-go cycle of the Argentine economy and fuels chronic inflation.*

1. The chronic trend toward shortage of foreign exchange is a characteristic of early stages of industrialization, as the process of industrialization itself requires significant amounts of imports (raw materials, components, and especially capital goods).
2. Foreign exchange for such imports cannot be supplied by industry because of the lack of competitiveness due to above-mentioned inadequate exchange rate.
3. According to the theory of international division of labor, these requirements of foreign exchange should be supplied by the most favored resource. This is indeed the case of oil-exporting countries, at least while oil lasts. However, with agriculture several problems arise. Contrary to industry, agriculture has increasing costs with volume: each acre more distant from the best areas, and even there,

each additional ton per acre, requires more investments, more fertilizers, etc., than the prior one.

4. Socially, the country needs industry and intensive agriculture. Extensive agriculture, such as practiced in the Argentine pampas, would absorb only a *small fraction of the work force.*
5. Agriculture means food, and food, in rich countries, calls for self-sufficiency; no country likes to depend on another country for such a critical resource. Therefore, grain and meat markets shrink, and in the long run there is no future for the corn exporting nations. Argentina's only trade opportunities left are (a) the continuing failure of USSR agriculture; and (b) occasional droughts or other climatic catastrophes (such as in the United States, 1988). There is still a significant need for food in poor countries, but without major international assistance this will not constitute effective demand for nondeveloped exporting countries, due to the inability of poor countries to pay cash.
6. Modern technology constantly diminishes the agricultural countries' natural advantages of soil and climate, because it allows many crops to grow on less fertile lands. Even if the cost advantage of being able to avoid such high technology still exists, the competitiveness of agricultural countries diminishes.
7. Other reasons for the prices of natural resources to lag behind industrialized goods are climatic risks, dependence on natural cycles, and difficulty of storing. This leads to timing rigidities, that weaken the bargaining power. Prebish (1963) explains why *the advantages of division of labor are not split evenly among the participants.*
8. Classic theory of international division of labor assumes *static* comparative advantages. Unless *dynamic* processes are considered —Kaldor's (1964) "*learning by doing*"—there will be no way out of the status quo, i.e., no development. Understanding the dynamics of industrial productivity requires what Maruyama (1985) calls a "morphogenetic mindscape," i.e., the belief that *not all processes will tend automatically to equilibrium*, and that our universe is full of nonequilibrium-seeking systems.
9. Once the foreign exchange shortage sets in due to the process of industrialization, policies are implemented to restore balance of payment equilibrium. These policies are both (a) demanded by the IMF and (b) promoted by local economists and politicians, who sometimes go *beyond IMF orthodoxy.* As shown, this often makes the counterdevelopment loop start again.
10. In addition to the chronic foreign exchange shortage mentioned above, a specific feature of developing countries must be empha-

sized: the notion of bottlenecks. Classical economy deals mostly with homogeneous levels of availability or scarcity of goods. Developing countries, however, with less visibility, predictability, and flexibility in the allocation of resources, may lack certain items which, though not significant by themselves, can stop whole lines of production. Often, such scarcity is caused by lack of foreign exchange and/or foreign credit.

11. In other words, once bottlenecks set in, the only way out is a lower level of activity, or the provision of the item causing the bottleneck. This takes time and, above all, foreign exchange. Thus, the foreign exchange shortage becomes the most significant bottleneck of all.
12. To counteract foreign exchange shortage, foreign funds are attracted by means of extremely high yields in dollars. Such yields are based on the assumption that, for some time, the exchange rate will be stable. When this assumption weakens, these funds will fly away as quickly as they came, but all at once and at the worst moment, causing havoc in the exchange market.
13. Thus, reactive strategies of national as well as international speculative investors, will trigger generalized capital flight, even by bona fide citizens wanting to protect their savings. This is an extreme case of deviation-amplifying mutual causal processes, where objective signals of *current inflation and probable devaluation* are intermingled with *perception of danger, lack of confidence, and anger*, all reinforcing one another.

The Issue of Inefficiency

Several aspects related to efficiency need to be pointed out:

1. Inefficiency, as defined above, should not be exchange rate–dependent, but rather be mostly a function of physical productivity. However, when prices are used as an indicator of efficiency, and those prices are compared internationally, misunderstandings may arise.
2. Efficiency is a condition for development: according to orthodox theory, *unless* you are efficient you will not be able to export, and without exports you will not be able to develop. At the same time, efficiency is a *result* of development: underdevelopment causes all sorts of inefficiencies.
3. Classical economics has a way out of this dilemma: lower the exchange rate of your local currency, until you are competitive at the level of efficiency that prevails. This will mean a very low standard of

living for the average population. However, such is the price of inefficiency.

4. When, for natural reasons (see item 9 in The Issue of the Theoretical Model, above), one highly efficient sector of the economy exists, its product becomes the major export item. Economic dogmas and poor performance of regulations in developing countries prevent differential exchange rates, or at least major differentiating fiscal actions (selective export duties, etc.). Thus, the equilibrating function of the exchange rate does not work.
5. In Argentina, following the line of international division of labor, one of the major points of orthodox economics is the so-called inefficiency of the industrial sector. The orthodox view *mistakes inefficiency for lack of competitiveness.* Inefficiency is assumed to be measured by the inability of local industry to compete abroad in international currency terms. However, this is a reflection, not so much of the efficiency level, but of the exchange rate level.
6. This does not mean that the efficiency issue is irrelevant; the differential exchange rate that should be established for industry vis-à-vis the most favored natural resources would be less if the efficiency were higher. So that, even if efficiency is not the main culprit as seen by the orthodox theory, nevertheless it is an important issue not to be disregarded.
7. Inefficiency does exist, and is often caused by mismanagement. To an even greater extent, it derives from the structural context. In other words, efficiency and development are two aspects of the same process: the *dynamic process of gradual development with joint efficiency improvement.*

The Issue of Inflation

Inflation causes a violent struggle for income, and at the same time, its main cause is precisely the violent struggle for income.

Why does inflation have such a devastating effect on social conflict? Several causes can be highlighted:

1. Chronic inflation, that for many years has stayed above 100% per annum, means that the local currency has ceased to function as unit of measurement. A country without a currency that functions as such is a country without stable values and without economic order.
2. Different theories (or, rather, types or cases) exist as to how inflation starts and grows; in Argentina, with said continuing inflation, *all* those theories apply. The classical explanations of demand-pulled and fiscal deficit–caused inflation play therefore a significant role, as

in any type of economy. However, in the Argentine case, the SBC-specific causes that follow are in our opinion more crucial and worth explaining, and are the ones highlighted in Figure 14.

3. Once inflation sets in and stays, positive feedback forces appear: *past* and particularly *expected* inflation induce supply-pushed and inertial price increases.
4. When, due to expected inflation, purchasers rush to buy and sellers prefer to wait and see, *the equilibrium–seeking classical price theory does not work. Thus, price formation occurs mostly in a monopolistic mode*, but without the economy of scale of true monopolies.
5. With continuing high inflation, huge swings in relative prices occur, because it is sufficient for any sector—labor, manufacturing, exporters, pensioners, etc.—to "lay still," i.e., to be unable to follow inflation, for a couple of months or even days, in order to loose income in "real terms."
6. By far the most significant cause of relative price variances originates with the mechanism that started the inflation process in the first place: the maxidevaluations originated by the cyclical shortage of foreign exchange. Goods that are subject to foreign trade (*transable goods*) and those that are only handled domestically (*nontransable goods*) are affected in a totally different way. This difference causes huge shifts of income from the cities to the interior, from industry to agriculture, from salaried personnel to corporations and vice versa. These erratic and significant shifts in relative prices make different sectors of the society temporarily favored at the expense of all others. Such ups and downs cause a fierce struggle for income: memory of the "ups" make the "downs" unacceptable. This can easily lead to political violence (Richardson, 1986) and raises the question of who benefits from, is served by, or "owns" the socioeconomic system (Flood, 1989; Jackson, 1989; Schecter, 1989).
7. Inflation usually combines with erratic interest rates, which sometimes exceed inflation (highly positive rates in real terms) and often are way below inflation (negative rates in real terms). In the first case, a *transfer of income from debtors to creditors* occurs. Many of those who used to apply their funds to production, find it more profitable to lend them in the financial circuit, with the State being the main borrower. In the second case, *the income transfer is from creditors to debtors.* This means that individuals cannot save, and it erodes the most classical possibility of the middle classes social ascent.
8. Inflation complicates most transactions, deterioration being proportional to the time frame of the transaction. In Argentina, this has been partly solved by all sorts of indexation clauses, but many

inequities remain. In addition, such *remedies tend to perpetuate the problem.*

Conclusions

What should be the result of a morphogenetic analysis of the Argentine economy and its sociocultural background? Mainly, it should determine (a) whether the system tends to equilibrium or to disequilibrium; (b) if the latter, whether the system is in (or heads toward) a crisis and, in that case, to analyze or forecast the characteristics of such crisis; (c) whether that crisis may be reabsorbed by the system or will end in catastrophe; (d) what can be done to enhance the chances of survival; and (e) what lessons taken from this process can be useful to other people.

The preceding analysis made it clear that this system does indeed tend toward disequilibrium: deviation-amplifying processes are much more numerous than deviation-counteracting ones.

As the continuation of deviation-amplifying processes ad infinitum is impossible, the answer to the second question is equally clear: the system is bound to head toward a crisis. Only its characteristics remain to be seen and how the system will emerge from it, if at all.

In early 1989, when the present study was started, this was a matter of opinion; after 40 years of inflation, in the last 15 years rarely below three digits per annum, some persons could think that this disequilibrium could go on forever, whereas others (ourselves included) thought, on purely cybernetic basis, that the system was bound to explode. By early 1990, when the final version of this chapter was written, the system did explode, first in coincidence with an impending change of government, and then during the initial efforts of the incoming one. On several occasions inflation reached 3% per day, the exchange rate multiplied by 10 in one month, and the overall situation resembled Germany's hyperinflation of 1923. Under those conditions, the understanding of morphogenetic economics and its sociocultural background became a matter of survival.

This issue of survival puts in the forefront one of the major dilemmas of most change processes: the choice between gradualism and "big bang"—i.e., dealing with all variables at once. The most important conclusion, after analyzing an SBC such as Argentina in terms of morphogenetic economics, is that gradualism is not applicable.

The main advantage of gradualism is that advancing step by step allows a gradual learning process. Its traditional disadvantage is symmetrical: the other parties learn too, and the forces opposing change get stronger with each partial step. Be that as it may, one even more important issue appears. In the case of a "system of vicious circle systems," where deviation-amplifying mutual causality prevails, advancing gradually—acting on just a few variables at each time—cannot break the vicious circles; the interconnections and the feedback and feedforward processes are too strong.

This brings us to the concept of crisis. Argentina seems to have come to a turning point, one of the essential characteristics of a crisis. In this case, it is more than a political, cultural, or economic crisis; it is all that, embedded in a crisis of identity, very much in Erikson's (1972) terms.

Resolution of such a crisis will not mean breaking loose from all the characteristics described. As indicated by Starn (1976), a crisis usually occupies an intermediate area between "revolution" and "continuity." It implies "certain ongoing organic processes, but no equilibrium; a decisive conflict, but no total revolution." It does constitute a drastic change of trend, but the framework of democratic institutions may and should be preserved. Whenever democracy was replaced by authoritarian regimes, the cost in terms of civil liberties, republican learning processes, and even lives was extremely high, whereas the benefits—the changes effectively achieved—were mostly superficial.

Seen from the historical viewpoint described in the section on sociocultural characteristics, this is a growth crisis turned into a survival crisis. It is the case of the Greek "hybris" mentioned by Miguens (1989) and Thom (1976): the breaking point when previous, far too favorable circumstances cease to exist, and the regulatory mechanisms fail.

Following Thom's subjectivism, we may say that Argentina is in crisis because the social actors have realized that the breakdown of its regulatory processes is a menace to its existence. In this sense, crisis may be a condition for progress; "either it degenerates into catastrophe, or it is finally reabsorbed" (Thom, 1976).

Reabsorption means that the awareness (by the social actors) that the country reached said turning point will allow sufficient changes of social behavior, in time, to avoid the disintegration of the system. As Morin (1976) said, "the crisis creates new conditions for action." Or, as McLuhan put it, "breakdown is a potential breakthrough." The problems encountered by the first steps of the newly elected government of Dr. Menem seem to indicate that such a breakthrough is not easy.

Another conclusion of our morphogenetic analysis is that the change process will not take place "by itself": it will have to be "managed" because positive feedback does not provide autogenerated remedies. But one of the difficulties of developing countries is precisely to "manage effectively," especially in the public sector. The dangers of "overdoing it," of abandoning essential public strategies or, on the other hand, of manipulating variables that should better be left alone, of mismanagement, or of changing things in the wrong direction, are significant. Fine-tuning may be difficult in the beginning, and many a change process that "went too far" may have to be redressed in a second stage.

In addition, such management must adapt to local culture and characteristics. As Maruyama (1961 and 1980) pointed out, different mindscapes and different national cultures will originate distinct causal relationships, and this will affect said management styles.

The task will not be easy. A society is not a mere combination of variables; the preceding diagrams are not intended to give that impression. Those variables, as well as their interrelations and feedback-feedforward processes, do not occur in a vacuum, in a mechanistic mode. On the contrary, they are strengthened or weakened by social actors with vested interests in the change processes. Power relations define most of the outcomes of such processes, and each of those outcomes will have actors who stand to win and those who stand to lose.

To assume that the complex problems of a complex system as described would have a simple and clear solution would mean misunderstanding the issue of complexity. Change processes of such complex nature cannot be expected to be performed by the government alone. Only a critical mass of social actors, combining pluralism with coherence, and led by the example of honest and capable leadership, may bring about the changes required and break the vicious circles that define this system. Understanding the full implications of morphogenetic economics and morphogenetic cultural processes may be the first step.

References

Aguinis, M. (1988). *A country of fiction* (in Spanish). Buenos Aires: Planeta.

Diamand, M. (1973). *Economic theories, development and independence* (in Spanish). Buenos Aires: Paidos.

Diamand, M. (1978). Towards a change in the economic paradigm through the experience of developing countries. *Journal of Development Economis, 5*.

Diamand, M. (1986). Overcoming Argentina's stop and go economic cycles. In *Latin American political economy*. Westview Press.

Diamond, M. (1988). *Towards overcoming the restrictions to Argentine economic growth* (in Spanish). Buenos Aires: CERE—Centro Estudios de la Realidad Economica.

Erikson, E. H. (1972). *Adolescense et Crise, la quete de l'identite* (in French). Paris: Flammarion.

Flood, R. L. (1989). Liberating systems theory: A summary and literature review. *Proceedings of the 33rd Annual Meeting—International Society for Systems Sciences.*

Geyer, R. F., & van der Zouwen, J. (Eds.). (1982). *Dependence and inequality. A systems approach to the problems of Mexico and other developing countries.* Oxford: Pergamon.

Herrscher, E. G. (1986). Business and industrial systems in developing countries: The problem of images and values. *Proceedings of the 30th Annual Meeting—Society for General Systems Research.*

Herrscher, E. G. (1987). The cause-effect loop in developing countries. *Proceedings of the 31st Annual Meeting—Society for General Systems Research.*

Herrscher, E. G. (1988a). Cause-effect loops as explanation of underdevelopment. *Human Systems Management, 7*, 375–378.

Herrscher, E. G. (1988b). Mutual causality in developing countries. *Systems Practice*, *1*(3), 305–311.

Herrscher, E. G., Balicchi, E., Barcaglioni, A., Oviedo, S., & Szklowin, C. (1989). Change in systems and change of systems, the case of certain undeveloped countries. *Proceedings of the 33rd Annual Meeting—International Society for Systems Sciences.*

Jackson, M. C. (1989). The critical kernel in modern systems thinking. *Proceedings of the 33rd Annual Meeting—International Society for Systems Sciences.*

Kaldor, N. (1964). *Exchange rates and economic development. Essays on Economic Policy* (Vol. 2). New York: Norton.

Kovadloff, S. (1987). *Towards an imperfect future* (in Spanish). Buenos Aires: Botella al Mar.

Labourdette, S. Agulla, J. C., Feimann, J. P., Floria, C., Korn, F., Mallman, C. A., Mora y Araujo, M., Nino, C. S., & Vizer, E. A. (1989). *Argentina at the crossroads* (in Spanish). Buenos Aires: Tesis.

Luna, F. (1985). *Conflicts and harmonies in the argentine history* (in Spanish). Buenos Aires: Belgrano.

Maruyama, M. (1961). The multilateral mutual causal relationships among the modes of communication, sociometric pattern and the intellectual orientation in the danish culture. *Phylon—The Atlanta University Review of Race & Culture, First Quarter.*

Maruyama, M. (1963). The second cybernetics: Deviation-amplifying mutual causal processes. *American Scientist*, *51*, 164–179.

Maruyama, M. (1980). Mindscapes and scientific theories. *Current Anthropology*, *21*(5), 589–608.

Maruyama, M. (1985). Mindscapes: How to understand specific situations in multicultural management. *Asia Pacific Journal of Management*, *2*, 125–149.

Maruyama, M. (1986). Morphogenetic economics: Change-amplification by causal loops. *Technological Forecasting and Social Change 29*, 205–213.

McLuhan, M. (1968). *War and Peace in the Global Village.* New York: Bantam

Miguens, J. (1989). Personal communication.

Morin, E. (1976). Para una crisiología. In *La notion de crise* (in French). Spanish version (1979) Buenos Aires: Megápolis.

Prebish, R. (1963). *Towards dynamics of Latin American development* (in Spanish). Mexico. Fondo de Cultura Economica.

Richardson, J. M. Jr. (1986). Explaining politic violence: A dynamic modeling approach. *Proceedings of the International Federation of Automatic Control (IFAC)*, Cleveland.

Romero, J. L. (1956). *Argentina: Images and perspectives* (in Spanish). Buenos Aires: Raigal.

Schecter, D. (1989). For whom and to do what? Questions for a liberating systems approach. *Proceedings of the 30th Annual Meeting—Society for General Systems Research.*

Starn, R. (1976). Metamorfosis de una Noción. In *La notion de crise* (in French). Spanish version (1979) Buenos Aires: Megápolis.

Thom, R. (1976). Crisis y Catástrofe. In *La notion de crise* (in French). Spanish version (1979) Buenos Aires. Megápolis.

van Gigch, J. P. (1986). Explaining creativity through metacreation and paradigm displacement. *Proceedings of the 30th Annual Meeting—Society for General Systems Research.*

van Gigch, J. P., & Pipino, L. L. (1986). In search of a paradigm for the discipline of information systems. *Future Computing Systems*, *1*(1), 7–97.

3
The Role of Engineers in Japanese Industry and Education—An Industrial Sociologist's View*

KENJI OKUDA

The number of Japanese companies with manufacturing facilities in the United States and West European nations has increased markedly in recent years. But this only serves to remind us of the many cultural and social differences that continue to exist between Japan and industrialized Western countries. One striking example is the difference in the roles of engineers and frontline operations in the factory. In Japan's case, the social distance between graduate engineers and operators is, by and large, remarkably small. Engineers wear the same uniforms as operators. And they have their desks at the shop site, in most cases right alongside the foreman's desk.

The narrowness of this social distance between graduate engineers and frontline operators is even more conspicuous in comparison with examples from many developing countries. Engineers in those nations demand from the start that they be allowed to work in a private office away from the production site. They seek a high post from the very outset, such as assistant to the president.

The role of engineers in many Japanese companies differs considerably from that in either the industrialized Western nations or the developing countries. This chapter focuses on the unique relationship between engineers and operations in Japanese industry.

Engineers as Sociologists

It is widely acknowledged that the high productivity of Japanese manufacturing enterprises results from extensive factory automation or robotization. One must not overlook the fact, however, that success in

---

* This chapter first appeared in *Journal of Japanese Trade and Industry*, 5, 1983 and is reproduced with permission.

automation is itself a result of close cooperation between engineers and operators at the factory level.

Consider the automation of rolling work in the steel industry. The success or failure of automation depends on the availability of accurate data on the differences in rolling methods resulting from material quality, the subtle bending of rolls caused by rolling, roll expansion due to high temperature, roll wear from repeated rolling, the effects of cooling water, and so on. Engineers receive this data from operators and sort it out, analyzing causal relationships and establishing correlations in the form of numerical formulas. Only when this is done, it becomes possible to automatically control the job. In other words, successful automatic control can be achieved by combining the practical experience of frontline operators at the production site and the scientific analysis of engineers.

Another case in point is the robotization of automobile assembly lines. Most assembly-line robots have been designed and manufactured by engineers on the basis of the suggestions or desires of assembly workers. For example, one painting robot was designed in response to the operators' desire to avoid inhaling thinner gas, which is injurious to the human body. By the same token, the work of filling the gap between window frames and glass was automated when mechanical engineers designed a robot for that purpose on the basis of suggestions from operators. Few automobile producers purchase assembly-line robots that have been developed by other companies specializing in the manufacture of robots.

Thus most of the robots on the assembly lines have been designed on the basis of suggestions made by operators themselves. It is frequently said that modern mass production deprives workers of opportunities to express themselves, and that low worker morale is but a reflection of this. On the assembly lines of the Japanese auto industry, however, robots have become a means of self-expression for operators.

Of course, installing robots on the line is only one of the many steps that must be taken. The robot must also be taught the correct work procedure. On Japanese assembly lines, teaching robots is one of the more important jobs for frontline operators. Each operator is encouraged to acquire the ability to break down his traditional manual work into computer programs and input these into the robot. This ability differs fundamentally from the ability to do conventional manual work. Dividing manual work and reassembling it into a more efficient procedure requires a capacity for logical thinking. Put the other way round, operators must be able to process information. Engineers have an important role to play in helping operators acquire this skill.

In addition, operators are required to learn how to keep the robots in good working order. This ability to do maintenance work is essential, since product quality cannot be maintained unless the robots are kept working accurately. The same is true of all automated facilities. Today, operators make it possible to turn out high-quality products by preserving the accuracy of mechanical equipment. To do so they must correctly understand the structures and operating principles of the equipment they handle and the control systems. In addition to the traditional skills required for their jobs, they need the ability to think logically and process information.[1]

Operators cannot express themselves in modern automated factories dominated by a network of complex control systems unless they equip themselves with these sophisticated skills. Engineers play a vital role in supporting the operators' efforts to acquire such new abilities. If an operator fails to achieve this he may be relegated to a position where he would be little more than another of the numerous parts of the automated system. He would find himself in the degrading position of, in effect, being used by the robot.

The current trend toward robotization is here to stay. But operators will still be able to express themselves, even in the age of automation, if they succeed in improving their skills. Conversely, operators will be placed in the position of serving the robot and will find themselves increasingly frustrated if they fail to improve themselves, or if their employers do not invest in their self-improvement.

Thus we stand at a crossroads. Many Japanese enterprises have chosen the first road and continue to make positive efforts in that direction. I have the greatest respect for the tremendous contribution Japanese engineers have made to these efforts. In this sense, they are no longer technological engineers but rather sociological engineers.

Operators often amuse themselves by giving pet names to robots. In some cases robots are taught to do simple calisthenics, and "join" operators in these workshop exercises, which usually form an introductory part of the workday with the emphasis on safety. Clearly, Japanese workers regard the robot as a visible product of their own self-expression and therefore do not consider it a threat to their jobs. This may be taken as an expression of the tendency of the Japanese people at large to combine work and play.

---

[1] Research and Development Institute of Vocational Training, Employment Promotion Projects Corporation, *Development of Human Resources in Projects of Technological Innovations*, the Printing Bureau, the Ministry of Finance, Japan, 1983. This research project, begun in 1981, has the financial backing of the Ministry of Labor. The writer is the project leader.

Developing the Abilities of Engineers

The above discussion has left out one important question about the engineer—namely, his role as economist. To ensure efficiency in production activities, the engineer must acquire various management techniques including skills in process management, inventory management, and cost management. Space limitations prevent a detailed discussion of this subject here, but it is an essential ingredient in the making of a good engineer.

To sum up, then, the engineer must possess the following three sets of attributes: (a) technological engineering, (b) managerial economics engineering, and (c) sociological engineering.

Abilities (a) and (b) require logical thinking and can be acquired through systematic education at academic institutions. However, sociological engineering requires abilities that are difficult, if not impossible, to acquire through formal education. Under practical circumstances, an engineer needs social skills to be able to provide operators with the technical information they need and help them understand it in ways appropriate to their individual abilities. This kind of skill must be acquired by individual engineers through on-the-job experience. In Japanese industry, activities aimed at developing engineers' abilities thus naturally emphasize the acquisition of social skills, and it is accordingly important to create an educational environment conducive to such acquisition through experience.

Of course, this does not diminish the importance of acquiring practical abilities in the course of an engineers's education in technological and managerial economics engineering.

Technical education and introductory education on management techniques are critical for newly hired engineers. The standard practice in Japan is for company managers and specialists to offer a series of lectures on the present state of any technology unique to the company, the firm's pressing themes in technological research, and the direction it intends to move. In addition, new engineers are taken on tours of production sites and research laboratories to further their understanding of the total company effort. There is nothing peculiar about this education. In fact, it or its equivalent is provided by practically every Japanese corporation.

Japanese companies believe, however, that the practical technological engineering abilities required of the engineer can be developed only through hands-on experience after his assignment to a particular section to perform a particular job. For example, the design engineer develops his skills in the process of trying to incorporate various ideas into his designs without losing track of the cost requirements in order to satisfy the needs of particular customers to the greatest degree possible. His practical abilities are improved through constructive criticism of his drawings by his superiors or through their encouragement and assistance in making the designs more functional and workable at the manufacturing site. In short, practical engineering abilities, as opposed to formalistic knowledge, can best be developed on the job.

For this reason, it is widely held in Japanese industry that those in supervisory positions in the shop must be good teachers for their subordinates. It takes a long time, however, before such on-the-job education bears fruit. Moreover, the supervisor must give each of his subordinates a job that demands of him greater technological expertise than he already possesses if he is to improve his abilities.

This means, of course, that the subordinate always faces the possibility of failing at his new task. Yet even if he fails, he can still learn useful lessons from the experience, and thus improve his abilities over the longer haul. It is therefore essential that supervisors have the courage to give their subordinates demanding jobs that will help them improve themselves; they should not fear failure.

This is also why it is absolutely vital that managers' performance be evaluated from a long-range perspective. If only short-term performance is emphasized, the manager will be less positive about developing the abilities of his subordinates. He will not give them demanding jobs for fear he might be forced to take responsibility for their failures and, as a result, be given a low performance rating.

In Japanese industry the emphasis is on long-term performance evaluation. This lets managers foster the abilities of their subordinates under extended programs.

Some Japanese academics criticize Japanese companies for making light of short-term quantitative performance evaluation, arguing instead that the long-term approach described above is not scientific. One must recognize, however, that success or failure in human development is too important a question to be decided solely on the basis of short-term quantitative evaluation.

The improvement of engineering abilities must be addressed from a long-term viewpoint. In the gradual process of skill development, engineers are, whenever necessary, sent to university as special researchers; they are also encouraged to publish their research at academic conferences or participate in projects involving not only academicians but engineers and researchers from other companies. Their abilities are improved in these and other ways. Human development must be undertaken consistently over a long period of time, without excessive preoccupation with the evaluation of quantitative achievements.

The principle of learning through work should be observed even more rigorously with sociological engineering skills, beginning with introductory in-house education.

This initial orientation for new engineers is generally completed in one to three months, after which they are assigned to particular sections. Assignments are made based on their own requests as well as on the observations of personnel experts during the orientation period and aptitude assessments during interviews. Evaluations by the senior engineers who served as instructors during the orientation also carry great weight.

In all cases, the new engineers are, in principle, first assigned to production sites. Assignments to other places, such as technical and planning sections or quality control sections at the head office or technical staff sections at factories, are generally avoided. Thus, as a general rule, engineers spend the first few years of their career on the front line. This is considered the time to put primary emphasis on education.

This belief that engineers with a university education still need an additional one to two years of education may give the impression that Japanese companies do not accord much value to formal schooling. Far from it. What it really indicates is a belief that workshop experience is indispensable to the development of sociological engineering abilities.

Many Japanese, in fact, are of the opinion that a university education has clear limitations insofar as the sociological realm is concerned. They see such education as best suited to acquiring a logical system of knowledge; in other words, universities teach only what can be acquired through logical thinking. The life of the "common man" at the production site, however, is not always logical. He is not accustomed to expressing his thoughts to the elite class in a logical form. By getting directly in touch with workers' lives and sharing their lives, engineers can learn about their mentality.

I have said here that the common man is not accustomed to expressing himself logically. This does not mean, however, that workers are the intellectual inferiors of engineers. Rather, they possess a profound wisdom about life and a deep pride in themselves. Once they are given an opportunity to show their pride and use their wisdom, they exhibit unsuspected energy. Mental activity, be it sustained concentration on maintaining and improving product quality or the creation of new ideas for improving work methods and raising production efficiency, cannot be carried out effectively without the strong energy of the common man. Engineers must be able to read correctly what individual workers have in mind and give them opportunities to fully demonstrate those basic desires that they find so difficult to express in logical form.

It is also an important task of engineers to give frontline operators technical information related to their jobs through day-to-day contact in the shop, and thereby give them confidence in their own work. Needless to say, classroom teaching methods do not serve the purpose. What is needed is a practical teaching method fitted to the concerns and abilities of individual workers.

In addition, engineers must try to encourage and help operators to develop their own ideas and present them in the form of specific suggestions. In this way, operators are offered an opportunity to experience the pleasures of self-expression. There is no denying that these and other "sociological engineering" techniques are a major source of the vitality of Japanese enterprises.

Before concluding, I might add that close cooperation between engineers and operators is not achieved through ordinary educational activities nor through so-called behavioral science measures. Certain economic and social preconditions must be met if a satisfactory relationship is to be established. As I stated at the outset, the social distance between engineers and operators in Japanese industry is traditionally very narrow. Moreover, both are members of the same union, which means that wages are calculated along the same principles. In addition, the wage gap is far smaller than in the industrialized Western nations. Engineers and operators both enjoy similar standards of living. Consequently, they share similar lifestyles, and find it easier to understand each other. This is another important fact that must not be overlooked.

Before World War II a wide differential existed between white-collar and blue-collar wages. The social distance was also wider than it is today. It is no exaggeration to say that the abolition of discrimination between white-collar and blue-collar workers through postwar trade union activities has had a sweeping effect on Japanese industry. This is probably not something that had been anticipated by the trade unions, but they have had tremendous influence nonetheless. I disagree with the view that Japanese unions have socially less power than their counterparts in the United States and other Western nations. But that is a topic for another article.[2]

[2] This point is discussed in some detail in my *Japanese Pattern of Management and its Vitalization*, Japan Productivity Center, 1982.

4
Thinking in Networks to Avoid Pitfalls of Managerial Thinking

GILBERT J. B. PROBST and PETER GOMEZ

Why a Holistic, Integrated Problem-Solving Method?

Managerial problem situations have become more complex recently and human thinking often appears no longer to keep pace with the complexity. Psychologists, biologists, communication researchers, and ecologists have meanwhile proved that the human mind produces forms of mental models of our world that often are simplified and reductionist pictures of the "real" situations. All we receive are small windows through which we comprehend our world.

Perceived or constructed realities no longer fit designing and controlling complex situations, such as in a development project, in a political environment of town or regional planning, in a multinational company's strategic planning, in detecting early warning signals in a publishing market, etc. (cf. Dörner, 1981; Gomez, 1984; Gomez & Probst, 1987; Lorange & Probst, 1990; Vester, 1976).

Logical fallacies are continuously arising in business, particularly in approaching and dealing with problem situations. These logical fallacies described thereafter—a result of our practical and consulting experience as well as a literature search (see above)—ask to be counteracted with a holistic, integrated, problem-solving method.

In an environment of increasing complexity, managerial thinking is often short of requisite variety by using an overly simplistic and one-dimensional approach. Logical fallacies as described in this paper often have a crucial impact for successful management. These logical fallacies led to the development of the problem-solving methodology as presented in the following in the form of a case study. The rationale for designing the methodology in the proposed way is given elsewhere in detail (Gomez & Probst, 1987; Ulrich & Probst, 1988). Here, its elaboration in a practical context aims at providing the reader only with

---

Reprinted with permission from G. J. B. Probst, P. Gomez, "Thinking in Networks to Avoid the Pitfalls of Managerial Thinking," *Human Systems Management*, 8(1989)3, pp. 201–212.

the overall picture and allowing him a first intuitive grasp. The case study chosen concerns a chain of bookshops, a retail business with different branches. The majority of our readers may have an intuitive feel for that business as we all are interested clients.

Delimiting the Problem

Logical fallacy: "Problems exist objectively and need only to be clearly formulated"

As the well-known management consultant Peter Drucker (1974) stresses, we never deal with facts, but always with opinions about facts. The perception of reality differs from observer to observer, from problem-solver to problem-solver. Problems are not simply given but are delimited and defined as problems by somebody. Depending on the point of view, perspective, values, social position, etc., the same situation can be defined differently (cf. Ben-Eli & Probst, 1987, Ulrich & Probst, 1988; Watzlawick, 1981.)

Our education system actively fosters the assumption that problems are given. We present pupils with problems that they have to solve, but the finding or interpreting of problems is omitted or prohibited.

In problem situations in business management we often find not only innumerable shades of interpretation, but also irreconcilable standpoints (e.g., in strategic issues, policy-making, etc.). If we look at a hospital, for example, from the viewpoint of the doctor, the administrator, the politician, the citizen, or the patient, its purpose will be seen as very different in each case. It makes a major difference to define a hospital's purpose as

responsible for preventive medicine, health education and maintenance of health, or
responsible for remedying injuries to health where they occur.

Business management problems are not something objectively given that can be unambiguously, correctly, and unanimously defined. Light must therefore be shed on situations from the different interest positions

It is therefore essential to

take the observer's point of view into account
adopt different points of view and mark out boundaries
always reconsider a situation and try to understand it from as many sides as possible.

and perspectives. Starting off from *one* problem definition is a mistake that we all too easily make.

If one starts from the position that the main objective of a book chain is to maintain or improve the profit position, the first obvious perspective for delimiting the problem is the managerial one. But it would be wrong to limit ourselves to this single aspect. An unfavorable profit position might only be a symptom of a deeper-seated problem. The profit situation also has to be seen in the larger context of the business responsibility of the bookseller, who fulfills an important sociopolitical function.

For these reasons, in the first step of the methodology the problem situation must be illuminated from several different perspectives and an appropriate interpretation found. The purpose of bookselling can be described as

earning an adequate revenue or profit (management)
securing optimum sales of books (publisher)
maintaining a wide range of books available (politician)
earning an adequate return on capital (investor)
providing favorite reading material (consumer)
providing jobs for qualified professional staff (economist)
providing an interesting and demanding job (employee).

If the problem situation is viewed from these different perspectives, completely different variables and interrelations appear as important.

Establishing a Network

Logical fallacy: "Every problem is a direct consequence of a single cause"

Our training, education, and experience lead us to think predominantly in simple, causal, and linear chains. For every event, effect, or change we seek a cause. Decision trees and organizational charts represent good examples of linear thinking. In a decision tree, we work step by step in a linear manner from cause to effect, until we arrive at the "last" decision point. Organization charts lead us to think in terms of hierarchical relationships from the top downward, instead of in networks. This also is closely and directly linked with the "scapegoat theory," for ultimately in the event of an accident at work, an ecological catastrophe, or a financial disaster, we need a guilty party to which we can reduce the cause. It is convenient to think in terms of such trivial relationships.

But today's problems in businesses, hospitals, etc., do not present themselves like this at all. Problems are not the consequence of a single

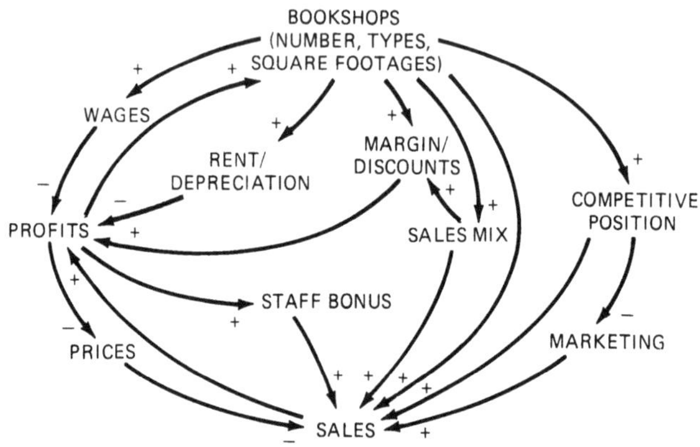

FIGURE 1. Network for the bookshop chain from the business management viewpoint.

cause. Nor can they be restricted to a single job description, marketing action, leader attitude, etc. Problems pay no heed to our organizational categories in training and education, or to business structures (Probst, 1985; Ulrich & Probst, 1988). For example, fish dieback in a section of river is not the problem of the biologist, the politician, the water bailiff, a business, the sewage experts, etc. Rather, we have to deal with a network of innumerable interrelationships and interactions in response to many different influences, secondary effects, threshold effects, accumulations, etc. Assigning one-to-one relationships and reducing things to cause-and-effect is no longer adequate in network systems. Although this logical fallacy of cause-effect thinking is obvious, we often have great trouble in seeing the critical interactions in a business context.

Although each individual connection seems "clear," it is still difficult to see strategic product-market goals, investment projects, earnings and profit targets, profitability considerations, capital volume, reward systems, etc., in a network. But these not only affect a large number of relationships and interactions, they also affect themselves in a circular or cyclical manner (cf. Lorange & Probst 1988, 1990).

> It is therefore essential to
>
> draw networks and "see through" them
> understand and analyze relationships, interactions, and cycles
> understand networks in their properties and as entities.

From the managerial viewpoint, a network construction may start at profit and the variables influencing it, these being the number and design of sales outlets, the competitive situation, and sales. A minimal

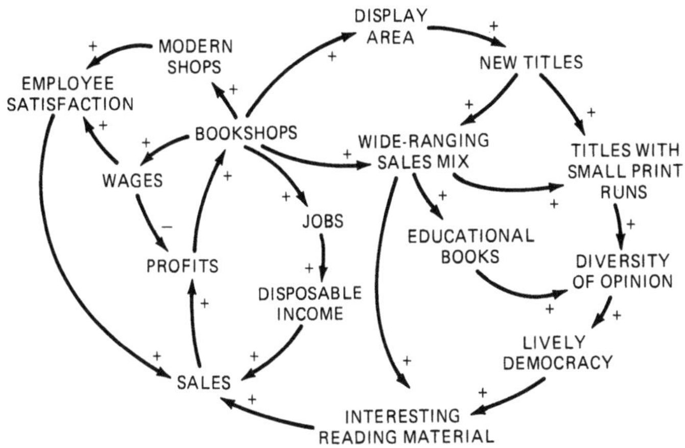

FIGURE 2. Network for the bookshop chain from the social viewpoint.

network model from the managerial aspect, which nonetheless possesses a certain degree of informativeness, might look like Figure 1.

The interdependencies of the network, where + denotes a positive feedback or reinforcement and − a negative feedback or stabilization (cf. Gomez & Probst, 1987; Maruyama, 1963; Ulrich & Probst, 1988), need to be commented on briefly. An adequate profit makes investment in individual bookshops possible, either in terms of renovations or of opening new outlets. New or renovated bookshops allow the sales mix to be better presented, and a more complete and balanced sales mix to be stocked. The mix of goods can also be used to bolster the position of those titles with larger margins, which in turn leads to increased profits and so enables investment in the network of sales outlets. Strengthening the shop network also improves competitiveness, and therefore sales and ultimately profits as well. On the other hand, more bookshops means higher wage and salary costs, and so a decrease in profits. The network therefore has an equilibrium, which should in the long run lead to an increase in profits.

As already illustrated above, the managerial perspective is not the only viewpoint. The network for the same problem situation seen from the sociopolitical viewpoint could be modeled as shown in Figure 2. Of course, this model can be extended considerably as has been shown elsewhere (Gomez & Probst, 1987, p. 37).

Comprehending the Dynamics

Logical fallacy: "All that is needed to understand a situation is a 'snapshot' of the actual position"

Even when we are aware of the relationships and interactions in social problem situations, it is difficult to avoid falling into conceptual pitfalls. We are tempted to analyze the state of a problem situation at a particular moment without understanding its dynamics. But it is only the dynamics that make a problem situation really complex for us. Due to the *nature* of the interactions a system behaves in a way that for us is incomprehensible, unplanned, or contrary to intuition. The interactions can compound a process within the system. Such self-reinforcing relationships have a *destabilizing* effect. The relationship structure inexorably "explodes" due to growth or "freezes" due to contraction. An obvious example of a positive interaction can be found in the principle of compound interest. The larger the principal, the greater the interest, and so the larger the principal becomes. . . . But a positive interaction can frequently be found in both directions. The mutual relationships between confidence and creditworthiness are an impressive example of this in the banking and credit business. The greater the confidence, the greater the creditworthiness, so the greater the confidence. . . . Conversely, a decrease in confidence leads to declining creditworthiness and therefore also to a similar, i.e., *positive*, interaction. This explains a lot of bank collapses, regardless of whether genuine and unavoidable financial difficulties were involved, let alone the courts. A negative interaction between two (or more) variables exists when the relationships ultimately operate on the same starting point in dissimilar ways. If the price of an article rises, production will generally be increased, because it becomes attractive from a financial point of view to produce a lot. With higher production (and therefore a greater supply), prices tend to drop as a rule. This cycle has a stabilizing or balancing effect. The interactions also have *different strengths, significances, and quantitative and qualitative properties.* Furthermore, social institutions have their "own time frame" inasmuch as some interactions take place very quickly whereas others are very slow. For example, bottlenecks may keep on occurring in production or in the warehouse, although the dependent relationships and sequences of events are well known. The market reacts to a new situation quickly. Businesses frequently do not take advance measures, and new actions only take effect in the longer term. Actions taken to intervene in the market, or changes in the qualitative aspect of the product mix, etc., are not infrequently characterized by little understanding of the time factor. If no effect can be established on the market of changes in production methods, new advertising measures, improved quality control, etc., projects are often abandoned prematurely or the measures strengthened without any awareness of the time delays and "working through" times. Because of this, we are then confronted by unexpected results, side effects, and "destroyed" or "disturbed" systems.

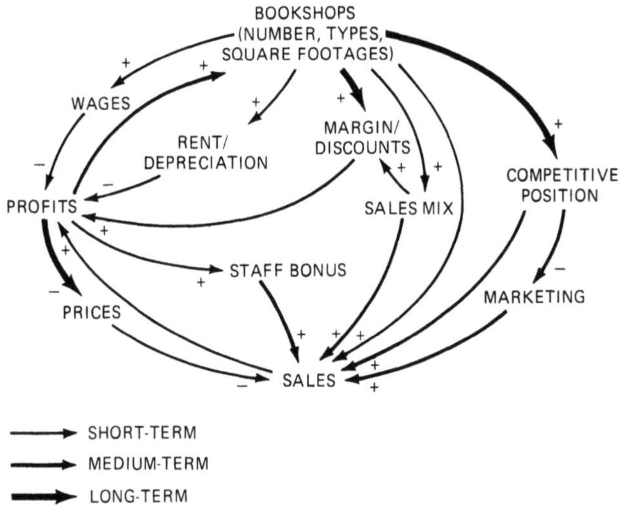

FIGURE 3. Time dependencies in a partial management network of a bookshop chain.

> It is therefore essential to
>
> recognize and understand stabilizing and destablizing relationships, interactions, and cycles
> analyze the strengths, significance, and qualitative aspects of relationships, interactions, and cycles
> include the time aspects in any consideration of a situation.

So far in the methodology, the central problem variable—the profit—has been set in the larger context of the network. The question now arises as to how this variable is influenced by other variables, and with what time horizons and intensity. The answers to these questions will form the starting point for determining effective control interventions to solve the problem.

The dynamics of the problem situation are above all the results of the time interdependencies in conjunction with the individual variables. Portraying this *time aspect* in the network is essential, since this is the only way in which certain behavioral patterns can be explained. In the network drawn from the managerial viewpoint, the time interdependencies can be shown as in Figure 3.

For example, expansion of the bookshop network has an immediate effect on wages and rental, or depreciation costs, and therefore on profits. But it usually takes more than a year for an expansion program for the chain, initiated on the basis of increased profits, to be realized

Effect on ↓ / of →	Network of bookshops	Wages	Sales mix	Prices	Sales	Competitive position	Rent/depreciation	Marketing	Margins/discounts	Profits	Staff bonus	Active sum AS
Network of bookshops	–	3	2	1	3	3	3	1	2	2	0	20
Wages	0	–	0	0	2	1	1	0	0	3	2	9
Sales mix	1	1	–	0	3	2	1	1	2	2	0	13
Prices	0	0	2	–	3	1	1	1	3	3	0	14
Sales	2	1	1	1	–	2	3	2	1	3	2	18
Competitive position	3	1	0	0	3	–	2	2	3	2	0	16
Rent/depreciation	2	0	0	0	0	0	–	0	1	3	0	6
Marketing	0	0	1	0	2	1	0	–	0	1	0	5
Margins/discounts	2	1	2	1	1	2	1	0	–	3	0	13
Profits	3	2	1	0	0	2	1	1	1	–	3	14
Staff bonus	0	1	0	0	2	0	0	0	0	1	–	4
Passive sum PS	13	10	9	3	19	14	13	8	13	23	7	

FIGURE 4. "Paper computer" for the bookshop chain.

and the same time horizon must be expected for the effect of a changed sales mix on sales. Several years usually pass before the expansion of the bookselling business is reflected in a discernible strengthening of competitiveness.

The study of the *intensity of the interrelations* between the variables involved is made using a kind of "paper computer" (cf. Ulrich & Probst, 1988; Vester & von Hesler, 1980), which reveals the active, passive, critical, and inert elements within the network. Control interventions in passive and inert variables hold little promise. The critical variable offers far greater opportunities, but also involves the danger of unforeseen reactions if one proceeds incautiously. Finally, the active variables are the ideal subjects for control interventions—if they can be influenced at all.

The paper computer in Figure 4 shows the intensity of the relationships between the variables in the managerial model. To pick out one example, the number and structure of bookshops have a large influence on wage costs, sales, competitiveness, and rent, but only a slight influence on prices and none at all on the staff bonus.

The paper computer analysis gives the following picture, with the most characteristic variables given for each category:

active elements: prices, network of bookshops, sales mix
passive elements: rent/depreciation, staff bonus
critical elements: sales, profit, network of bookshops
inert elements: staff bonus, marketing

What conclusions can be drawn from modeling the dynamics of the problem situation for possible control interventions? Of central interest are those variables identified as active elements in the paper computer and at the same time classified as quick-acting in the network (with the exception of prices, which are fixed by the publishers). A change in the sales mix proves to be a relatively fast-acting and simultaneously an effective measure. A change in favor of titles attractive in terms of margins leads directly to increased profits.

As already described, expansion of the network of bookshops takes longer, so there are no effects on profits until the medium term. But experience has shown that expansion and renovation is a reliable source of increased profits, so this measure is indispensable. The staff bonus also presents itself as a fast-acting measure. But as the paper computer shows, it has relatively little influence in the total network and therefore lacks the necessary leverage to improve profits. Finally, marketing efforts do not produce the great leap forward from the point of view of either the paper computer or the time dependencies. Good locations for passing pedestrians and a cleverly assembled sales mix are the secrets of success in the book trade.

Comprehending the dynamics of the problem situation has revealed two main points of application of possible control interventions, namely the sales mix and the expansion of the network of bookshops. Before these application points are further evaluated, the behavioral possibilities of the problem situation must be examined so that surprises can be detected early and either be exploited or countered.

Interpreting the Behavioral Possibilities

Logical fallacy: "Behavior is predictable; all that is needed is an adequate information base"

We often think that we can predict the results and behavior of complex social phenomena as if they were simple machines, and that because information removes uncertainties, predicting behavior is simply a matter of how much information we have. And if we do not have a piece of information, it is merely a question of time until we receive the information to make everything predictable. "We can't do it yet but it's only a matter of time until the information is available" is a conviction often heard from management.

There have hardly ever been as many researchers into the future, planners, forecasters, etc. as there are today. Many of our ideas, models, methods of action, or decisions are based on this notion that behavior or circumstances can be predicted. The future is regarded to a certain extent as something preordained, determined in advance, and inevitable, which merely has to be ascertained by using all the information. Examples of this are the predictions by many researchers into the future and the disappointment caused when the predictions are not completely correct (the researchers are often misinterpreted because a clear prediction is desired, although they themselves warn against this and wish only to offer possible pictures or visions of the future for discussion). Similarly, with business forecasts we frequently find such fundamental assumptions, methods of action and disappointments in connection with business planning. People forget that what we have here is an interlocking network system, very many parts of which are affected by any change and which also acts back upon itself. But in network situations, by no means all the information is available, and consequently it cannot be assimilated, regardless of the possibilities of future information technology.

Rather, information is generated by the interactions within the network. Predictions are therefore continually being overtaken by events. Analytical studies on predicting are therefore not only rendered ineffective by human thinking equipment and our capacity to conceptualize, but are also put into question by the property of belonging to a network. An overall integrated approach that considers the system as a whole is therefore imperative. Although the result may be sketchy and only exists in terms of rough outlines, it leads to greater appreciation than detailed analyses of whichever parts can by examined. The detailed analysis of individual parts is worthless if we do not recognize the relationships between the parts. (cf. Hayek, 1967, pattern prediction; Probst, 1987).

Exact predictions in complex social systems are impossible. For this reason, it makes more sense to obtain a wider, integrated picture of future behavioral possibilities as a whole than "wrong" predictions of a precise section, analyzed in detail. Knowledge of the functional interconnections within a business allows scenarios or behavioral possibilities to be played through and correspondingly to become active. By doing this, we take account of both the process aspect and a system's time properties. We are striving for a dynamic approach in which no immutable fundamental assumptions are made for the sake of the model.

Determining factors	Probable scenario	Pessimistic scenario
Prices	Price maintenance will continue, and the pricing policy of the publisher will not change	Price maintenance will be discontinued (consumer protection initiative)
Network of bookshops	The continuous private and public development of the infrastructure for shopping locations provides new locations and allows experiments with new shops	Expenditure on infrastructure will be cut back sharply, making the opening of new locations increasingly difficult
Wages	The wages structure will remain in its present form. Wages will increase in step with retailing as a whole	Wage negotiations will become tougher and lead to a generally higher level of wages
Margins	Present-day margins (discounts) can be maintained	The publishers and whole-salers impose a reduction in margins, to the detriment of booksellers
Sales mix	The ratio of paperbacks to hardbacks will only change slightly in favour of the former	Paperbacks and bestsellers will exert more and more pressure on hardbacks

FIGURE 5. Scenarios for selected determining factors.

It is therefore essential to

- become aware of and receptive to the behavioral possibilities of the system
- develop possible "patterns" or scenarios for the future
- carefully consider and evaluate the opportunities and dangers, and also the strengths and weaknesses, in the various contexts.

In this step of the methodology, scenarios of possible future developments are therefore produced for the major parts of the network and the network as a whole. A few probable and pessimistic scenarios are set out in Figure 5 for some of the central variables. Recognition of these influences enables a directed course of action to be followed, which is the aim of the next step of the methodology.

Determining the Design and Control Possibilities

Logical fallacy: "Problem situations can be 'mastered'; it is simply a question of effort"

Just as we cannot predict the actual course of a game of football, or the trainer cannot control the events on the field by taking the right actions, we are subject to limits in every social system. This applies to a game of soccer as well, although we know the rules and there are only 22 players on the field. The precise behavior of each player and the interactions can be neither predicted nor mastered. Seen abstractly, every game of football displays the same organization, but the actual course of each game is a unique event that is never repeated in the same way. The idea of being able to master problem situations, or the world in general, is closely linked with a technocratic view of the world. We think we can organize and control whole natural and social entities in the same way as we build and control machines. The complexity that results from a network, however, not only leads to the fact that we can never know and predict everything, but also to the fact that we cannot master these systems. The behavior of every part of a network influences and changes every other part. This behavior is in turn dependent on the structure of the whole, i.e., on the interactions between all the parts. Since we can never know everything that we ought to know in complex systems, complex problem situations cannot be "mastered." However, we can lay down *rules* that lead to an order, and detect individual critical variables for stability or change. The innate dynamics of a system, its inherent organization, *must always be included* in the organizational and control activities. Order, stability, and change arise from the interaction of many people and man-machine interfaces.

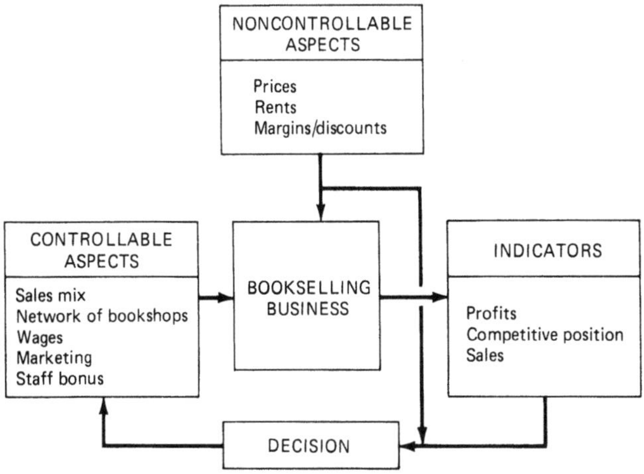

FIGURE 6. Simple control model for a bookselling business.

However, order cannot be traced back and reduced to individual organizers and exercisers of control (cf. Probst, 1987). As in a game of soccer, the pattern of order that emerges is the result of a large number of networked actions.

> It is therefore essential to
>
> carefully elicit all possible controllable and uncontrollable aspects from the viewpoint of the observer
> draw the connections to other variables
> design strategies that make sense in the context and are of value.

As every expert on retailing knows, the possibilities of improving profits are very limited and heavily dependent on developments beyond his own influence. It is therefore of great importance to carefully evaluate the problem solver's own design and control possibilities in this step of the methodology.

On the one hand this means crystallizing controllable aspects, i.e., those problem areas where targeted actions are possible. On the other hand, it must be ascertained how surprises in those problem areas outside the problem solver's own sphere of influence, and therefore not controllable, can be avoided. The main aim is to take preventive measures to nip unfavorable developments in the bud by means of suitable countermeasures. Finally, those variables that show whether the set objectives have been reached, namely the indicators, must still be determined. The control possibilities for the problem situation in the bookselling business are summarized in Figure 6.

Shaping the Design and Control Interventions

Logical fallacy: "A 'boss' can push any problem solution through into practice"

We usually start from the assumption that solutions to managerial problems are worked out, planned, selected, and introduced on a project basis. Every action in a social system produces changes. Other people become suspicious, feel threatened or disturbed, expectations change, defense mechanisms are built, measures taken, things disregarded, etc. Frequently just analyzing or tackling a problem can lead to changes, perhaps even to the resolution of the defined problem. The system seeks to avoid disturbances to an equilibrium—often even if this equilibrium is undesirable. The idea that "solutions" can be implemented by taking systematic action is closely linked to the linear, single-cause attitude.

Emphasis is placed on the manager as an individual, as a boss, and little attention is paid to the circumstances and conditions of the overall entity. Often we also think we can draw up a final organizational concept, a management model such as management by objectives, a plan, etc., and introduce it. This founders on the inherent activities, reactions, or advance measures of the system itself.

Taking action *against* the system is almost always wrong. Measures that catalytically utilize and strengthen the trends, forces, and processes, etc., within the system are more successful, and have greater scope for development in the long term. Changes should not be bludgeoned, but if possible should "grow out" of the system as a whole (cf. Probst, 1987). This requires a certain tolerance toward the forces in the system, but also the acceptance that not everything can simply be done in the way we intended and forced upon the system. Problems have to be *solved* by a change arising from within the system itself, so that the problem is no longer "produced." However, solutions tend mostly in the direction of removing problems by means of imposed solutions, in other words of solving a problem in the sense of it no longer existing or being visible.

Nevertheless, the structure of the situation generally remains, so that problems can recur. Only the symptoms have been made to disappear. A solution of this nature frequently inclines toward actions at the expense of other people (profit/loss situation), which represent "sham" compromises or which try to ignore the problem as much as possible.

It is therefore essential to

pay attention to the "innate patterns" of the system that is being acted upon (take the history of the system into account)

make use of the forces and specific properties of the system
allow something to happen at the right place at the right time.

This step of the methodology is centered around rules (cf. Gomez & Probst, 1987; Probst, 1981, 1985, 1987; Ulrich & Probst, 1988) for optimizing control interventions, which among other things stipulate that the best possible use should be made of the inherent dynamics of the problem situation (cf. Gomez & Probst, 1987, p.30). If optimization of the sales mix is chosen as a control intervention, the following rules can help in shaping the interventions:

Make use of the inherent dynamics and synergies of the problem situation. A bookselling business can incorporate other information media, and become an information center with books, newspapers, data bases, new media, etc. Moreover, combinations of media can be offered covering topics of particular attraction, e.g., video and audio cassettes and periodicals on the same subject as well as books.

Find a harmonious balance between conservation and change. Change the sales mix in the direction of an information center or specialist bookshop gradually, so as to cautiously introduce the customers to the new structure. For example, set up a separate "New Media Corner" first, demonstrating how books fit in with the new media.

Encourage the autonomy of the smallest unit. The individual bookshop should be as autonomous as possible in setting its own sales mix. It should match its range of items offered and its presentation to the particular characteristics of its circle of customers. As well as optimizing the sales side, this also provides corresponding motivation for the branch manager.

Rules for judging control interventions

1st rule: Match your control interventions to the complexity of the problem situation
2nd rule: Direct your measures at the active and critical influencing factors
3rd rule: Use stabilizing feedback to avoid uncontrolled developments
4th rule: Make use of the inherent dynamics and synergies of the problem situation
5th rule: Find a harmonious balance between conservation and change
6th rule: Encourage the autonomy of the smallest unit
7th rule: Increase the learning and development capabilities with every problem

Assessing possible control interventions on the basis of the systemic rules for shaping interventions leads to the selection of a problem-solving strategy. This must be put into practice in the final step of the methodology.

Realizing and Further Developing a Problem Solution

Logical fallacy: "With the introduction of a solution, the problem can finally be laid to rest"

Organizational questions, planning operations, complete decision processes in sales, research, and production, etc., are often handled and completed as if they were projects. Once an annual plan, an organization structure, etc., has been drawn up, the task executed, and the objective reached, the "problem" can be laid to rest. However, as we have already seen, all actions and interventions lead to changes. How often do preliminary studies in the business, or discussions with staff, lead to changed attitudes, judgments and thereby to new situations (cf. Greiner, 1972; Lorange & Probst, 1988, 1990). Perhaps the "problem" is already a different one afterward. But every individual step in the problem-solving process has different effects. Definitive solutions do not exist, and instead new questions, problem definitions, or situations arise constantly. Business operations are also continually changing, which again poses the question of whether the problem solutions or measures are still appropriate. "Problem solutions" must be continually reassessed and adapted so that changes in the environment and system can develop harmoniously. This demands that a certain flexibility, sensitivity, and openness toward "new" problems be retained. Conflicts, mistakes, divergences, etc., should not therefore simply be avoided or suppressed; fluctuations and experiments should be allowed and observed, and any new problems discovered and developed.

It is therefore essential to

monitor the development of the situation
organize the problem solutions as flexibly as possible and with maximum learning possibilities
be sensitive and respond creatively to weak signals indicating new problem situations.

It is a characteristic of a good problem solution that it possesses the necessary flexibility not to become obsolete immediately when the first

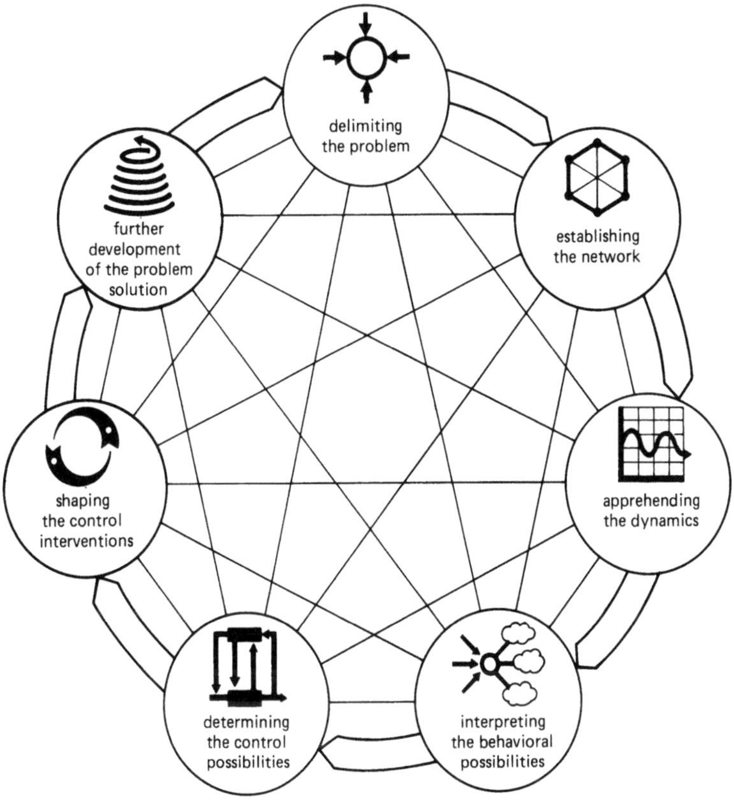

FIGURE 7. The problem solving methodology.

difficulties arise. Problem solutions should be shaped and introduced in such a way that they "repair" themselves by constantly adapting to their environment and improving. The process of evolution, which by means of constant mutations and a selection of suitable reactions leads to continuous further development, can serve as the guiding idea here. The following examples should illustrate this:

Deciding on the sales mix is not a once-and-for-all process. Instead, experiments must be carried out constantly on the presentation of books and on the addition of certain titles. This is the only way to optimize margins.

The relatively low investment required for experiments makes a bookshop ideally suitable for trying out new, smaller shop types and testing new ways of presenting articles. New ideas must be continually tried here, in order to slowly get closer to "Bookshop 2000."

Internally, the staff must be trained in how to simulate the effects of new presentation and sales methods on personal computers.

This step concludes the methodological action. It has led to solutions that hold out the promise of success. Above all, it has created the basis for dialogue among the staff involved in the problem-solving process, which allows a solution to be constructed step by step in a repeatable way. It is this repeatable construction process that often imparts the necessary motivation to carry out the measures decided upon. The group process for working out a solution has been stressed here, but from the didactic point of view the best method of learning the problem-solving process is to follow it in practice.

References

Ben-Eli, M., & Probst, G. (1987). The way you look determines what you see. *Cybernetics and Systems*, *18*(4), 276–284.

Dörner, D. (1981, July). Ueber die Schwierigkeiten menschlichen Umgangs mit Komplexität. *Psychologische Rundschau*, 163–179.

Dörner, D. (1984). *Lohausen—Vom Umgang mit Unbestimmtheit und Komplexität.* Bern: Huber.

Drucker, P. (1974). *Management.* New York: Heinemann.

Gomez, P. (1984) Early warning in business: A system approach. *Journal of Applied System Analysis*, *2*, 65–78.

Gomez, P., & Probst G. (1987). *Vernetztes Denken in Management.* Die Orientierung Nr. 89. Bern: Volksbank.

Greiner, L. (1972). Evolution and revolution as organizations grow. *Harvard Business Review*, (7/8), 37–46.

Hayek, F. A. von. (1967) *Studies in philosophy, politics and economics.* London: Routledge & Keegan.

Lorange, P., & Probst G. (1990). Effective strategic planning processes in the multinational corporation. In C. Bartlett, Y. Doz, & G. Hedlund (Eds.), *Managing the global firm.* 144–163. London: Routledge & Keegan.

Lorange, P., & Probst, G. (1988). Joint-ventures as self-organizing systems. *Columbia Journal of World Business*, *22*(2), 71–77.

Maruyama, M. (1963). The second cybernetics: Deviation-amplifying mutual causal process. *American Scientist*, *51*, 164–179.

Probst, G. (1981). *Kybernetische Gesetzeshypothesen als Basis für Gestaltungs- und Lenkungsregeln.* Bern/Stuttgart: Haupt.

Probst, G. (1985). Regeln des systemischen Denkens. In G. Probst & H. Siegwart (Eds.), *Integriertes Management* pp. 181–204. Bern/Stuttgart: Haupt.

Probst, G. (1987). *Selbst-Organisation.* Berlin and Hamburg: Parey.

Ulrich, H., & Probst, G. (1988). *Anleitung zum ganzheitlichen Denken und Handeln.* Bern/Stuttgart: Haupt.

Vester, F. (1976). *Urban systems in crisis.* München: Deutsche Verlagsanstalt.

Vester, F., & von Hesler, A. (1980) *Sensitivity model.* Frankfurt.

Watzlawick, P. (1981). *Invented reality*; here in the original German version, *Die erfundene Wirklichkeit.* München: Piper.

5
Crossing Intellectual Boundaries:
Biology and Politics, Problems and Lessons

ALBERT SOMIT

Starting in the mid-1960s, a small handful of political scientists, understandably viewed as eccentric by even the most charitable or their colleagues, began to use biological[1] concepts and techniques in their efforts to better explain and study political behavior. Today, barely two decades later, the advocates of "biopolitics," as the movement was quickly dubbed, number several hundred, drawn from more than a dozen countries; the latest survey of the literature identifies over a thousand items, and biopolitics has been recognized as an "official" subarea of political science by both the International Political Science Association and the American Political Science Association, the discipline's two largest and most prestigious organizations.

This chapter addresses two questions: First, what has the biopolitical approach contributed to our understanding of political behavior? The second question is quite different but, at another level, perhaps even more important: What problems were encountered in, and what lessons are to be learned from, this experiment in cross-disciplinary fertilization, especially one involving such seemingly dissimilar fields? Before turning to these questions, though, I think it essential to describe very briefly both the background and the intellectual sources of this most recent effort to effect a marriage between biology and political science.

---

[1] Unless otherwise specified, I refer here to evolutionary theory, ethology, and sociobiology.

Background and Intellectual Sources

Previous Efforts to Develop a Biologically Oriented Political Science

There was, or course, a well-known and highly unfortunate attempt in the 19th century to use biological concepts to explain political behavior. As Darwin (or what was often incorrectly claimed to be Darwinism) achieved scientific acceptance, the concepts of evolution, natural selection, and "survival of the fittest" were promptly pressed into service both by those who resisted, and those who sought, the extension of governmental authority into economic and social spheres. The fact that advocates of diametrically opposed political philosophies could find persuasive support in evolutionary doctrine eventually discredited what we now call *Social Darwinism.* Regrettably, it also discredited the premise that biological concepts could be fruitfully employed in the study of social and political behavior. Even worse, it cast into disrepute the assumption underlying this premise—i.e., that human behavior was meaningfully influenced by our genetic makeup.

Looking back, the earlier quest seems to have been almost foredoomed to failure. First, the biology of the era was simply unable satisfactorily to explain biological, let alone social, phenomena. Second, many of those who rushed to apply evolutionary doctrine to social issues were unaware of the limitations and weaknesses of the concepts they were so enthusiastically borrowing; frequently, they did not even grasp the ideas involved. Third, as so often happens when those in one discipline seize upon developments in another, Darwinian theory was put to purposes for which it was never intended and forced to bear a burden of argument for which it was manifestly inadequate. The coup de grace was the embrace or "biology" by the proponents or racism, a group whose scientific ignorance was equaled only by the stridency with which its members proclaimed their views.

For these and other reasons, the inevitable reaction occurred. By the 1920s and 1930s, most social scientists drew a sharp line between man and all other forms of life. The behavior of other species was understood almost entirely in terms of biological inheritance (instinct); that of Homo sapiens was viewed as almost totally learned and having little, if any, relationship to our genetic legacy. Political man was treated as if he had no behavioral predispositions whatsoever (back to *tabula rasa*), and political and social behavior were seen as the product of learning and social conditioning, leavened by "intelligence" and spiced with a dash of "personality." So held the conventional wisdom.

The Revival of Interest in Biology

By the 1950s and 1960s this view came under increasingly severe attack. The way for the change was prepared by Freudian psychology. Although many of his disciples were reluctant to admit it, Freud's emphasis on the inherently irrational (or nonrational) nature of human behavior demanded, in the final analysis, a direct link between biology and human action, since any *innate* behavioral tendency has necessarily to be rooted in man's genetic makeup.

More important, though, were major advances in biology itself. Since these have been dealt with at considerable length elsewhere, they need only be noted here. Research in neurology, psychoneurology and psychopharmacology demonstrated beyond a doubt that human behavior—intellectual and emotional, as well as physical—can be influenced and even controlled by altering the physiological functioning of the body. Developmental biology forged a conceptual apparatus—the neo-Darwinian synthesis—increasingly capable of explaining animal evolution, natural selection, and speciation. Genetics was enriched by discoveries that simultaneously clarified the process whereby genetic instructions are transmitted from generation to generation and opened the way for human intervention in, and modification of, that process.

Perhaps the most decisive single factor was the transformation of ethology from a relatively obscure to an almost indecently glamorous specialization. Two ethologists, Konrad Lorenz and Nikolaas Tinbergen, became Nobel laureates; several ethological books—all stressing the manner in which an animal's behavior is influenced by its genetic legacy—made the best-sellers' list; and documentaries or fictional treatments of animal behavior became a regular feature of commercial and public television. Although the ethological materials were drawn almost entirely from studies of subhuman species, the moral, not always merely implied, was clear: human behavior, too, has it roots in our genes.

The impetus provided by ethology was given even greater, almost irresistible, momentum by Edward O. Wilson's *Sociobiology* (1975). Wilson's concluding chapter advanced the claim that the sociobiological principles and concepts he had utilized to account for insect and animal behavior could also be readily applied to the study of Homo sapiens. Soon, he promised, biology would provide a sound scientific basis for what we now call the social sciences. The promise may have been rash; it was assuredly premature, but it attracted extraordinary attention.

These developments, reinforced by an upsweep of concern over man's relationship to his environment, rekindled among many social scientists a desire to explore the possibility of utilizing biological concepts and techniques. Within political science, this experiment has been underway for about two decades. Similar enterprises have also been launched in sociology, social psychology, geography, anthropology, law, and economics. In short, the pendulum seems to be well along its return journey. We can only hope that the lessons of the earlier debacle will not be entirely forgotten.

The Contributions of Biopolitics to the Understanding of Political Behavior

The most important accomplishment of biopolitics, I would say, has been to achieve growing acceptance among political scientists of four broad propositions:

1. That, as ethologists and sociobiologists agree, human social and political behavior is to a significant degree influenced by our species' evolutionary history and the behavioral tendencies which are a product of that history; and that among these genetic tendencies are sociability, dominance hierarchies, aggressive behavior, violence, nepotism, xenophobia, reciprocal altruism, and the formation of small group alliances.
2. That human social and political behavior can be significantly affected and/or modified by (a) our physiological makeup and/or (b) changes in physiological functioning brought about by illness, stress, drugs, fatigue, and malnutrition, to mention only some of the more obvious possibilities.
3. That biological, physiological, and biochemical measures such as galvanic skin response, heartbeat rate, eye-blink rate, blood analyses, body posture, etc., can be used to assess emotional and attitudinal states and, it seems reasonable to conclude, behavioral potential.
4. That some of the most urgent policy decisions currently facing our society are those dealing with essentially *biological* issues—environmental pollution, genetic engineering, treatment of the terminally ill, population, abortion, food shortages, nuclear radiation, acid rain, and AIDS are among those that immediately come to mind.

These propositions identify, respectively, I should add, the research foci of the four major subfields generally recognized within biopolitics.

Given the sizable corpus of writing (articles, books, and papers) generated by those who study politics from a life sciences perspective, a complete review of the literature would require a volume in itself—a task which, in fact, is now underway. For purposes of this discussion, therefore, I will use a baker's handful of illustrative items picked, in part, to provide instances of work done in each of these subfields. My choices are admittedly arbitrary, and I can only apologize to the many colleagues whose research I have not been able to cite or, perhaps no less vexing, have found it necessary to describe with almost indecent brevity. I will begin with a fairly offbeat but intriguing study, selected not so much for its substantive importance but because it shows how a biopolitical approach can be utilized on the individual, personal level. The other examples will be drawn from research dealing with somewhat weightier matters.

Brain Lateralization and Presidential Behavior

Many, if not most, neuropsychologists now believe that, as a general rule, the human brain's left hemisphere specializes in analytical "logical" processes and the right hemisphere in holistic "intuitive" thought. William Kitchen has attempted to assay hemispheric involvement as manifested in presidential press conferences held by (then) Presidents John Kennedy, Richard Nixon, and Ronald Reagan. Kitchen found that Reagan and Nixon had more right hemisphere involvement than Kennedy; Kennedy more active left hemisphere processes than Reagan; and both ranked higher than Nixon on this score. Whatever else was learned, Kitchen's readers were undoubtedly reassured by the news that there was evidence of brain activity on the part of *all* three presidents, a matter on which some skeptics had expressed serious doubts.

Gender and Political Competence

According to Plato, women were fully qualified mentally and physically to participate as political equals in the *Republic*; Aristotle, voicing what has been the dominant (male) opinion, insisted that women were essentially lacking in the intellectual and personal attributes required to make sound political decisions. From Greek days onward, political practice has strongly favored the Aristotelian stance; even today, globally speaking, the cause of female political equality has yet to be won.

On this point, Glendon Schubert argues, both established practice and Aristotle are grievously wrong. The evolutionary history of the proto-hominids and then the hominids, he points out, surely entailed specialized roles for male and female, roles involving a differential utilization of the left and right hemispheres. Natural selection, working over countless generations, would thus lead to significantly dissimilar cognitive, intellectual and emotional processes as between the two sexes (more precisely, genders). Because they are different in this respect, women are more likely, given the opportunity, to make sound political decisions than men. "[It] is hard to believe," Schubert observes, "that women would not have done at least as well as the majority of male presidents of the United States during the Twentieth Century—and they can be expected to do far better than men during the Twenty-first . . ." (1991).

Rather ironically, many in the women's rights movement vehemently deny that there are *any* significant inherent intellectual or psychological differences between men and women. From their perspective, to concede any difference is to concede an inferior status or capacity.

Political Socialization

It has long been an article of faith among many political scientists that our political attitudes and opinions (and presumably the resulting political actions) are largely the product of childhood experience—i.e., the process called "socialization." According to the so-called primacy principle that undergirds this view, political orientations acquired very early in life not only persist, but also shape later political learning. Based on this belief, there has developed a sizable cottage industry of political scientists who study the political and social attitudes of subjects ranging from nursery and prekindergarten children to those in high school.

The idea that childhood socialization plays a key role in forming later adult attitudes and behavior has been challenged by two biopoliticians (Somit & Peterson, 1987). These critics point out (a) that even after decades of research, there is still no empirical evidence to support the theory; and (b) that research by Jean Piaget and Jerome Kagan, *inter alia*, dealing with the *biology* of neuropsychological, intellectual, and emotional development, raises grave doubts about the primacy principle. The evidence strongly suggests, in fact, that behaviorally meaningful political attitudes and opinions are *not* formed until the individual has matured—in the literal physiological sense—mentally as well as physically. If this contention is correct, political scientists will have to reconsider the accepted wisdom as to how, as well as when, we acquire our political values. Going one step further, Chong Phil Ra (1988) has used the evolutionary concept of punctuated equilibrium to explain the discontinuities (contrary to the tenets of the primacy principle) in political orientations and beliefs so often encountered in political socialization studies. These discontinuities, Ra points out, are predicted by punctuated equilibrium theory.

Stress and Elite Decision Making

History is replete with examples of disastrous decisions by civil and military leaders. Why such apparently inexplicable folly? Stupidity (a factor that cannot be entirely discounted) aside, it may be that decisions made under stress (fatigue, fear, sickness, time pressure, etc.) are much more likely to be "wrong" than those made under more normal circumstances. This is not a purely speculative or trivial matter. Poor political and military decisions have always had a substantial potential for mischief; today, in a nuclear age, that potential is truly unlimited.

One team or researchers, utilizing voice-stress analysis, has examined recordings of presidential speeches made during periods of international crisis to ascertain which statements, promises, threats, etc., are associated with evidence of greater or lesser stress. This technology can be used both to probe for evidence of stress and to pinpoint the specific topics or issues that seem especially stressful. By identifying the latter, it should eventually be possible to test the underlying thesis that stress affects the *quality* of decision making. It is a technique, of course, which could be applied to decision making at any political level—or to any other sphere of activity.

Popular Electoral Choice

How do voters decide between/among political candidates? Democratic theory postulates, and rational choice theorists contend, that this decision is (or should be) made by carefully weighing the policy positions and personal qualifications of the candidates. So seen, electoral preferences are essentially the outcome of a conscious, logical, analytic process. A contrary view, sometimes held by those sympathetic to democracy, as well as by its opponents, is that the process of electoral choice is fundamentally nonrational, and that emotions, bias, and prejudice play a determining role.

To test these competing hypotheses, a group of biologically oriented political scientists studied the reactions of control and experimental groups to television tapes of recent presidential campaigns. They found that, for many of their subjects, nonverbal communication (facial expressions, body language, etc.) played a greater role than the substantive arguments and speeches of the candidates.

From a biological perspective, these findings make excellent sense. Our primordial ancestors relied on nonverbal communications eons before they developed formal language (those who lacked the capacity to comprehend these signals were not likely to survive, let alone reproduce), and nonverbal communication remains an important, if usually "unconscious" component of our species' communicative repertoire. The democratic cause and the practice of democratic government would be strengthened rather than weakened by recognizing this biological reality.

Public Opinion Measurement

For the past several decades, much of political science research has revolved around the administration and interpretation of surveys, polls, and scales dealing with a variety of political issues, attitudes, and even behavioral "intentions." In most cases, the subjects are instructed to give a categorical ("I strongly agree," "I agree," "I disagree," etc.) response to a series of questions or statements.

Whatever the substantive merit of this approach, the so-called Stony Brook team has insisted that these traditional verbal responses, whether oral or written, are not as valid or reliable as magnitude scaling, based on human psychophysics. In this latter technique, subjects are asked not only for an oral or written response but, for example, to draw a line that would indicate by its length the intensity of the subject's feeling on that particular matter. The data indicate that such psychophysical measures are more reliable and valid than the traditional oral (or written) category scaling alone, and that the results are best when the two are combined. The technique, though quite suitable for experimental purposes, has not yet been adapted to mass public opinion surveys.

The Origin of the State

"Man is born free but is everywhere in chains," proclaimed Rousseau. "Those who believe themselves the masters of others are even greater slaves than the people they govern. How did this come about? I do not know. What can render it legitimate? That question I can answer."

As Rousseau was aware, one of the oldest issues in political philosophy is "How did the State (that is, organized political society) come into being?" Did the State originate in coercion and exploitation, as Marxian theory insists, or was it the result of general agreement and consent, as the "contract" theorists maintain? This is by no means an academic issue. The first theory denies the State any claim to legitimacy and justifies resistance and revolution; the second gives it a moral status and imposes upon the subject an obligation to obey—unless, of course, the State violates the terms of the contract.

Drawing upon the sociobiological concepts of inclusive fitness, reciprocal altruism, in-group cooperation, and intergroup competition, several writers have developed models presumably accounting for the evolution of political society as we now know it. In these models, the progression is from family to extended family groups; then, severe competition among these groups, involving efforts both to preserve and to disrupt the "balance of power," leads to the expansion of some groups into larger entities and eventually to the State. The sequence is plausible but the transformation seems unlikely to have been managed without a substantial degree of force and coercion, leaving the issue of "legitimacy" rather problematic.

Public Policy

So engrossed are we today with a deluge of biological problems ranging from abortion to AIDS that we forget that these are matters of relatively recent widespread concern. One of the pioneer biopoliticians, Lynton K. Caldwell, helped considerably to give these matters their present salience. Writing a quarter-century ago, he warned that "an explosion of biological knowledge and technology is raising questions of public policy which until recently were hypothetic, and were therefore from a practical point of view very unreal" (1964, p. 2).

Among the problems that Caldwell then identified, in addition to environmental matters, were "individual human behavior in the use of cigarettes, tranquilizers, narcotics, and alcohol . . . the biochemical control of personality . . . concern for the numbers and qualities of future population . . . and the issue of biological warfare" (p. 6). A prescient statement, indeed. A younger colleague, Robert Blank, has dealt in thoughtful fashion with the ethical, legal, and political aspects of genetic engineering and abortion, two issues very much in the foreground of public attention in subsequent years.

Toward a Truly Behavioral Political Science

As I indicated earlier, much of post-World War II political science research has entailed the utilization of surveys, polls, and questionnaires. In conducting these studies, political scientists have accepted expressions of attitude and belief, or of intentions to act, as a valid surrogate for real-life behavior. One of the ironies of the past few decades, in fact, is that so many of the social scientists marching under the banner of "behaviorism" have turned their backs upon behavior itself.

Here, I believe, biopolitics has already played a constructive role. Almost from the outset, its advocates have urged political scientists to adopt the research technique that contributed so much to the swift advance of ethology—the systematic observation of actual behavior in a real-life setting. How does homo politicus behave in his/her "natural" environment, whether that be the legislature, the courts, the executive branch, the polling place, the political convention—or wherever the Great Game of Politics is played? By example—the study of the development of authority patterns among preschool children, of judicial behavior in the Swiss courts, of city councils, and now of oral argument before the Supreme Court—as well as by exhortation, biopolitics may help in reorienting political science to the study of actual political behavior. If this alone is accomplished, biology will have significantly enriched political science.

Problems and "Lessons"

The development of a scientifically productive and professionally acceptable (two quite different propositions) biologically oriented approach to political science has been, as might be expected, attended by a variety of difficulties and problems. I will treat these under three headings—political, institutional, and intellectual—with the understanding that the latter two both overlap and interact.

To be sure, similar difficulties are likely to be encountered in almost all interdisciplinary efforts. The severity of the problems, though, may be a function of the "distance," intellectual *and* institutional, between the disciplines involved.[2] If so, we should remember that biology and political science not only deal with dissimilar subject matter/phenomena but that, in a university or research institute, the gap is perceived as so great that they are most invariably located in separate administrative units and report to separate officers. There may also be, as I will suggest, a further difference of mental set or "metatype," between their respective practitioners.

Political Problems

The first problem discussed under this heading, I should emphasize, is not endemic to interdisciplinary efforts generally but relates specifically to the *biopolitical* enterprise.

The stigma attached to Social Darwinism was multiplied manifold by the racial theories and, far worse, genocidal practices of National Socialism. Any attempt at a "life sciences" approach to politics now evokes, among many persons, an understandable suspicion, not to say fear. In Europe and in the United States, those who have been engaged in such efforts have been denounced as either practicing racists or as

---

[2] I can only speculate whether biologists seeking to apply political science concepts and research techniques to the study of biological phenomena would encounter either the same problems and/or at the same level of intensity. Given their respective places in the academic pecking order, that contingency seems rather remote.

unwittingly contributing to racism; there is the further criticism that biopolitical research, even *if* scientifically sound and objective in itself, is easily capable of distortion and of being put to evil political purpose. For this reason, its opponents say, *all* biopolitical inquiry is actually or potentially dangerous and should either be voluntarily discontinued or even formally prohibited.

There are, it seems to me, three possible rejoinders: First, a staunch defense of freedom of inquiry à la J. S. Mill; second, that there are no ulterior political motives and the research will be conducted with maximal scientific objectivity; and, third, that even if the findings are unpalatable, they may open the way for more realistic and presumably more promising policy options.

A second type of "political" attack may be based on religious or, in other instances, on ethical grounds. The basic objection here is to the biopolitical tenet, taken from ethology and sociobiology, that we must study Homo sapiens just as we would study any other species if we are to achieve an adequate understanding of human behavior generally and political and social behavior in particular.

From the perspective of the religious fundamentalist, such a notion directly contravenes the Old Testament, where the Book of Genesis clearly states that Adam was made in God's image. Taking the Bible literally, the fundamentalist regards it as sacrilegious to suggest a commonality between man and any other form of life. Because fundamentalists often also oppose the teaching of evolution, it is equally reasonable for them to oppose an approach to human behavior that takes its point of departure from Darwinism. To this type of objection there are but a limited number of responses—that the Bible is to be read as an allegory, that the Bible is ambiguous, that the Bible is not a historically accurate document, etc. For the true believer, none of these is likely to be very persuasive.

The ethical objection, on the other hand, is directed at the political dangers inherent in an ethological approach. Humans are born with inherent rights, so the argument runs, and must be regarded as ends in themselves. Consequently, they cannot and must not be treated as if they were "just another species." I fully agree. As I once wrote in acknowledging the force of this contention:

> It is one thing to study ourselves as if we were just another species. It is altogether different to act as if this were actually true. The Gulag Archipelago, no less than Dachau and Buchenwald, illustrates what can happen when governments and societies violate this injunction. Should we lose sight of the unique human claim to special treatment, we would, like Faust, have purchased knowledge at a truly exorbitant price.

A third type of "political" problem is posed by those who have a professional stake in the claim that our behavior is almost entirely learned. This has been the dominant tradition in sociology; it has also been the prevailing view in political science, both in the training of students and the practice of mainstream political science. Quite naturally, many in the profession look askance at any challenge to the established wisdom; nor are those who have made their reputations in, and who have devoted years of research to, such fields as childhood political socialization likely to be overly receptive.

As Kuhn and others have shown, attempts drastically to change long-accepted scientific paradigms frequently evoke obdurate opposition and bitter resistance. Over the long run, these historians suggest, the outcome may be determined as much by personal mortality and morbidity as by evidence and argument; in the short run, the battle is fought not only on an intellectual level but in the acceptance or rejection of articles, in appointments and promotions, in the awarding of professional offices and honors, and, no minor, matter, in the allocation of research funds.

Some fairly special circumstances, as I will shortly describe, made it somewhat easier for the biopolitical movement to cope with this type of professional political opposition than might have ordinarily been the case. Nonetheless, the problems were by no means trivial. For biopolitics, as well as for almost any other interdisciplinary enterprise, one maxim must be constantly kept in mind when dealing with resistance of this sort: *non illegitimus carborundum*.

Institutional Problems

With few exceptions, interdisciplinary movements have their origins and their settings within institutions of higher learning. Some of the most troublesome difficulties they encounter stem from that fact. Colleges and universities are organized on a departmental-disciplinary basis (for purposes of this discussion, the two terms can be used interchangeably) and scholars who are not clearly identified with a given discipline or department will frequently encounter severe difficulties with regard to appointment, promotion, and tenure.

As I mentioned earlier, many academics will find ample reason to reject any suggestion that their discipline's "paradigm" requires major modification. They also soon acquire a fine, territorial sensitivity to any actual or potential rival for departmental resources, whether these resources be students, staff, or funds. The consequences are all too familiar. During periods of institutional affluence, interdisciplinary programs will be lauded by the administration and tolerated by the faculty. When adversity strikes, however, the administrators soon fall silent—and the interdisciplinary ventures are the first to be cut, if not completely jettisoned. This is simply the reality of academic life, as many deans, academic vice presidents, and even presidents have ruefully learned.

Along with almost every other interdisciplinary movement, biopolitics was hard hit by the grave financial difficulties that American higher education encountered in the early 1970s. Most plans for new graduate programs combining biological and social science perspectives died on the drafting boards or, where launched, did not survive the ensuing fiscal surgery. And, of course, the bottom fell out of the job market for "orthodox" political scientists, let alone those admitting to such strange—and often suspect—interdisciplinary interests.

Fortunately, biopolitics was better situated than some of its interdisciplinary brethren (or sisters). Almost every one of the founding group was a full professor (or at least tenured) with already established reputations in political science. They could, therefore, pursue their new interests with relative unconcern about the job market, departmental opposition, or disciplinary skepticism, not to say, hostility. Consequently, they were able to give the movement a momentum and a continuity without which it might have otherwise faltered.

Younger practitioners, of course, had a more difficult time. As they "came on the market," they discovered that offers were made because of their training in the established "regular" fields and that their hard-earned biopolitical skills were rarely, if ever, seen as a significant asset. (In fact, at some of the more conservative departments they were probably regarded as a potential liability.) During most of the 1970s, too, promotions in political science were decided primarily in terms or publication dealing with orthodox, rather than exotic, subject matter. Only in relatively recent years, as budgets eased and as the new "field" achieved growing acceptance, has tenure been granted primarily on the basis of biopolitical publication.

With regard to publication, the biopolitical experience has probably been typical. Although at least half of the thousand plus items that constitute the biopolitical "literature" are articles (or books), relatively few of them are to be found in the "mainstream" political science periodicals. A biopolitics journal—*Politics and the Life Sciences*—was launched in 1982 and has since served as a major outlet. Nonetheless, it is gratifying to note that, over time, the discipline's leading professional periodicals have been increasingly receptive to biopolitical articles.

The lessons to be learned from the biopolitical experience are hardly novel. First, that the modern university does not provide a nurturing environment, to understate the matter, for programs which attempt to cut across departmental and disciplinary boundaries. Second, that those who elect to engage in such ventures do so at their own risk, especially the more junior members. And, third, that the junior individuals who join the enterprise (at least in its early years) would be well advised to make sure that they have another, more traditional, field of specialization in which they can demonstrate their qualifications for appointment, promotion, and tenure.

Of course, the ideal solution, for this and many other reasons, would be to drastically restructure the academy. That, however, does not seem to be a very practicable proposal.

Intellectual Problems

One lesson was quickly learned: the importance of solid, professional training in biology. The early proponents of biopolitics were, of necessity, self-taught. There was, consequently, sometimes a tendency to think, as a critic observed, "that the nonspecialist, the amateur dabbler, if you like, can easily grasp the main theories in biology." The practice of inviting professional biologists and ethologists to participate in our meetings quickly—and sometimes painfully—disabused us of any such notion.

Even where our grasp of theory and fact was relatively adequate, being autodidacts carried with it a further liability. This sprang, we discovered, from our near-total reliance on the printed word. Only by attending professional conclaves where work in progress is discussed and new ideas advanced and controverted—or, as a second-best option, by working closely with those who do so—does one get a real sense of where that discipline is today. Glendon Schubert (1989) has calculated that "when a person in one discipline attempts to make initial (and professionally guided) excursions into some other discipline, he/she typically cuts into the unfamiliar discipline about a generation . . . behind its contemporary cutting edge." That was pretty much our own experience.

As mentioned above, there still does not exist a formal doctoral (or even master's) program specifically designed to produce graduates competent in both political science and the relevant areas of biology. Training in biopolitics remains an ad hoc affair, requiring an individualized "package" of courses for each student and the cooperation of sympathetic colleagues in biology, anthropology, and other related disciplines. Although this has worked tolerably well, it is hardly ideal.

There was yet another intellectual problem and possibly a generic lesson for interdisciplinary ventures. We had to master biology; but, no less important, we had to learn to *think* like biologists, especially those who study animal behavior. By and large, political scientists are trained to think disjunctively, to look for single-factor explanations, and to look at political behavior in terms of stability and continuity, rather than change. (The literature of political philosophy offers abundant examples of the first; voting behavior studies illustrate the second; and most systems theory writing reflects the third.) In contrast, biologists (and I have ethologists primarily in mind) are more inclined to look for interactive processes, multiple causative factors, and ongoing adjustments to an often unstable and unpredictable environment.

More systematic graduate training in biology would, of course, help to close the gap between the two. The point here, however, goes well beyond the differences between biology and political science and relates to interdisciplinary activities generally. In borrowing concepts from another discipline, we should be alert to, and perhaps attempt to emulate, the manner in which the parent discipline approaches the phenomena with which it is concerned and the mental "set" that characterizes its practitioners. But that may be far easier said than done, an admission which brings me to my last, and perhaps most important, intellectual problem.

We know—or at least there is a great deal of evidence to suggest—that professions and scientific disciplines tend to be "self-selecting." That is, those with certain mental capacities and personality attributes tend to go into certain fields, those with different capacities and attributes into others. Approaching the subject from a different perspective, Maruyama and others have argued the existence of four basic, distinguishable modes of thought—sometimes called epistemologies, sometimes "mindscape types."

Whatever the terminology employed, the mindscape theory of conceptualization raises some interesting and potentially very troublesome issues for those concerned with the broader subject of interdisciplinary research and study. *If* individuals tend to manifest the characteristics of one or another of the four types that have been identified, the following empirical questions arise:

1. Do persons possessing these characteristics tend selectively to recruit themselves to given disciplines, or, alternatively, do disciplines tend to be heavily populated by practitioners who have a given "mindscape?"
2. Is the subject matter of a given discipline more successfully investigated by persons with a particular mindscape or, alternatively, are individuals who have a particular mindscape likely to be more successful in a given discipline than those who do not?

Should either of these two, and even more so if both, possibilities turn out to be the case, there are some obvious implications for a variety of interdisciplinary "borrowing" and interdisciplinary research efforts. I need mention only two. The first would be those situations where interdisciplinary activities might bring together individuals representing quite dissimilar "metatypes"; the second would be where individuals with a given mindscape, that associated with success in their own field, become engaged in an interdisciplinary effort involving a second discipline where some other type is more likely to be successful.

In short, the mindscape theory may help explain why some interdisciplinary programs have been or are more productive than others. Or, to put it in prospective terms, it may enable us to predict the combination of mental types and disciplines likely to yield the best results—and those which are less promising.

My aim in this essay, as I said at the outset, was to describe some of the accomplishments of biopolitics and to identify some of the problems encountered, and lessons learned, in that particular interdisciplinary undertaking. In the process, I now realize, I have also raised some larger questions and suggested a possible research agenda. I cheerfully leave the former to be answered, and the latter to be addressed, by my fellow participants in this volume and the many others who may have an interest in these matters.

References

Blank, Robert. (1988). *Life, death, and public policy.* De Kalb: Northern Illnois University Press.

Caldwell, Lynton K. (1964). Biopolitics: Science, ethics, and public policy. *The Yale Review, 54,* 1–16.

Kitchin, William. (1982). *Hemispheric specialization and political communication.* Paper presented at American Political Science Association annual meeting.

Ra, Chong Phil. (1988). *An ontogeny of political behavior: A punctuated equilibrium model of political socialization.* Ph.D. dissertation, University of Hawaii.

Schubert, Glendon. (1989). *Evolutionary Politics.* Carbondale: Southern Illinois University Press.

Schubert, Glendon. (1991). *Sexual Politics and Political Feminism.* Greenwich, CT.: JAI Press.

Somit, Albert. (1981). Human nature as the central issue in political philosophy. In Elliott White (Ed.), *Sociobiology and human politics.* Lexington, MA.: Lexington Books.

Somit, Albert and Peterson, Steven A. (1987). Political socialization's primacy principle: A biosocial critique. *International Political Science Review, 8* 205–214.

6
The Concept of System and the Paradigm of Complexity*

EDGAR MORIN

It is important to clarify the concept of system. Although the systems theory has shown the generality of the concept of system, it has not gone deep enough to discover the generative nature of systems.

As for the generality, all that was considered as matter in the 19th century is now considered as system (an atom, a molecule, a star, etc.). All that was considered as living substances have now become living systems. However, what is social has always been considered as a system. But this generality is not sufficient for recognizing the epistemological implications of the notion of system.

The systems theorists have thought that they have settled the problem. They believe that the new principle is *holism*, which seeks an explanation at the level of the whole and opposes reductionism.

However, I would like to point out that their holism is based on the same simplistic principle as the reductionism to which it opposes. As I discusses elsewhere (Morin, 1977, p. 101), the systems theory has neglected to scrutinize its own foundation and to clarify the concept of system. Thus the paradigm of system remains underdeveloped, atrophied, and stuck. The systems theory suffers from a basic weakness and tends to fall repeatedly into reductionistic, simplistic, distorting, and manipulating ruts, which it was supposed to have overcome and from which it should have freed us.

On the contrary, the understanding of systems requires a new principle of knowledge different from holism. We must see systems not only in a general term, but also in a generative way. We need a new paradigm. "Paradigm" is defined here as a set of basic relations of association and/or opposition among a limited number of key notions that command or control all our thoughts, discourses, and theories.

---

* Translated from French by Magoroh Maruyama.

The notion of system has always been basic in designating the entire set of elements constituting the whole. The notion becomes revolutionary only when it replaces the notion of thing or object, which was conceptualized as having a form and a substance, decomposable into primary elements, neatly isolatable in space, and subject to the external laws of "nature." The new notion of system breaks away from the classical ontology of object. We shall see that the object of the classical science is a segment, an appearance, a simplified and one-dimensional construct, mulilating and abstracting a complex reality that is rooted simultaneously in physical organization and psychocultural organization. We know the universality of the change that results from the notion of system in contrast to the notion of object. But what we must face is the radicalness of this change and the innovation which it might bring about.

The Paradigm of System

The Macroconcept

The question of the system cannot be decided in the part-whole relation, and the holistic paradigm forgets two very basic notions: interaction and organization.

The whole-parts relations must be mediated by the notion of interactions. It is incorrect to think that most systems consist of "parts" or "elements," as this view is based on the notion of materials. On the contrary, they consist of *actions* among complex units, which in turn consist of *interactions*. An organism does not consist of cells, but of the actions that take place among them. The set of these interactions constitutes the organization of the system. "Organization" is the concept that gives constructive coherence, rules, structures, etc. to the interactions and regulates them. In fact, the concept of system is a three-sided concept (Figure 1): system, which expresses the complex unity and the phenomenal nature of the whole as well as the complex of relations between the whole and the parts; interactions, which express the set of relations, actions, and feedbacks that are interwoven in a system; and organizaction, which expresses the formative character of

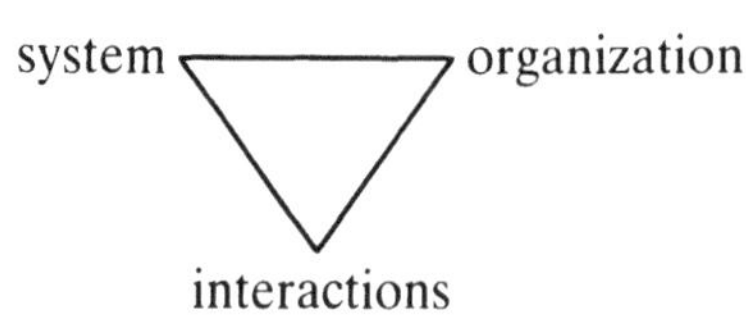

FIGURE 1.

the interactions by composing, maintaining, protecting, regulating, directing, and renewing them, thus serving as a backbone to the concept of system.

These three notions are inseparable. The absence of any one of them seriously mutilates the concept of system. It is a macroconcept. In contrast, we can now realize that the method of understanding by simplification, with which we have been educated, has provided us with atomic concepts instead of molecular concepts, static and isolated concepts of chemistry instead of organismic concepts that generate one another in the feedback relation of their interdependence.

The concept of organization originated in various sciences based on structure. But structure is a static concept that falls back more on the concept of order in the sense of invariable rules rather than on that of organization. It tends to reduce the process of the system to the structure that generates the process. It does not take into account the mutual feedback between the whole and the emergences.

In most of the physical and chemical systems and in all biological systems, the "organization" is active. It is "organiz*action*." It includes supply, storage, distribution, and control of energy as well as consumption and dissipation of energy in its work. The organiz*action* is a product of entropy (degradation of the system and of itself) and a product of negentropy (regeneration of the system and of itself). One must conceptualize the relationship between entropy and negentropy in a complex way. These two terms are not dichotomously opposed, but they are tied to each other (Morin, 1977, pp. 291–296).

We must conceptualize the organization (a) as a perpetual reorganization of a system that tends to disorganize itself; and (b) as a perpetual reorganization of itself, i.e., autoreorganization.

In living creatures, such an organization is doubly polarized: generativity (genetic organization containing the so-called genotype programming), and phenomenality (the organization of activities and behaviors of the phenotype). In other words, it is an organization that is auto-(geno-pheno)-reorganizing. Moreover, such an organization involves exchange with the environment. The environment is itself a macro-organization in the form of ecosystem (a biocenosis inside a biotope), and provides organization in the form of vegetables and animals as food, and the potential for organization in the form of information. It is a living organization that is at the same time the organization of closure (maintenance of integrity and autonomy) and that of openness (exchange with the environment or ecosystem). In this sense it is an auto-eco-organization. Thus from the simplest unicellular organisms to human societies, all organizations are at least auto-(geno-pheno)-eco-reorganization.

Therefore the problem of organization cannot be reduced to a small number of structural rules. From the beginning, the concept of biological and a fortiori social organization is a super-macroconcept, which is a part of the macroconcept system-interactions-organization.

Organization is a concept of a superior paradigmatic character. The paradigm of the classical science considered that explanation consists of reduction to order (laws, invariances, averages, etc.). We are not replacing order with organization, but are combining both into the systemic organizational principle as a nonreducible principle of explanation. The new principle includes disorder at the same time. The organization creates order (by creating its own systemic determinism) and disorder. On the one hand the systemic determinism can be flexible and allow for zones of uncertainty, play, and freedom. On the other hand the organizing work produces disorder (increase of entropy). In the organizations, the presence and continual production of disorder (degradation, decay) cannot be separated from the act of organizing. At this level the paradigm of organization involves also a new way of thinking. Nevertheless, the new way of explanation should not exclude disorder nor obscure organization, but most always consider the complexity of the relation shown in Figure 2.

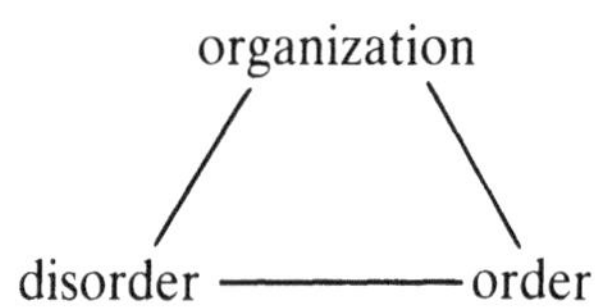

FIGURE 2.

The new paradigm includes uncertainties and antagonisms by combining terms that imply mutually. The new spirit of science, which began with Bohr, consists in improving the explanation, not by eliminating uncertainties and contradictions, but by recognizing them. It improves knowledge by clarifying the zone of shadow that exists in all knowledge, in other words by *improving* the ignorance, because acknowledged, duly noted, and well-researched ignorance becomes qualitatively different from the ignorance that does not know itself.

Finally, we must break away from the distorting notion that misconstrues the concept of system or organization by eliminating the notion of being or existence. I have attempted to show that the concept of self-organization generates being and existence (Morin, 1977, pp. 211–215). This is of crucial importance and it sets two types of thought in contrast: the one that functions only by obscuring the concrete beings and existences, by condemning them to all types of manipulation; the other that functions only by showing the reality of existential beings, which is of crucial importance as far as living creatures and human beings are concerned.

Thus, we see that a new knowledge of the organization creates a new organization of knowledge. A new paradigm, consisting of the interrelations among the elements as shown in Figure 3, replaces the old reductionistic and atomistic paradigm whose only principle of explanation is order.

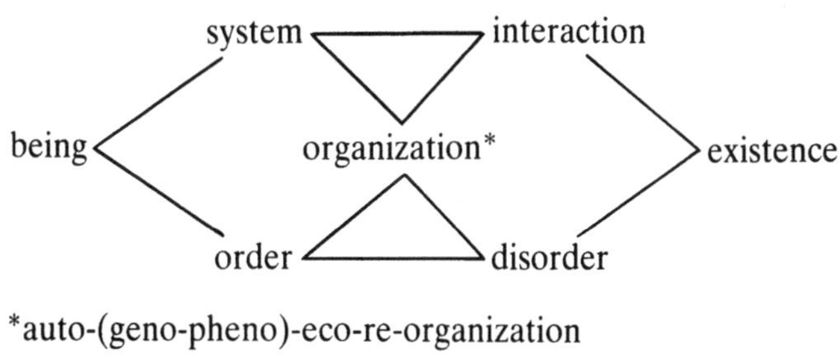

FIGURE 3.

Instead of the old solitary key word, we now have a macroconcept, not only of the molecular character but also with circular relations among the terms, in other words a macroconcept of a recursive character.

The Paradigm of Complexity

After the foregoing discussions, a fundamental term to clarify is *complexity*. Most frequently what is considered complex is the complicated, the entangled, or the fuzzy, which cannot be described because of the astronomical number of measurements, operations, and computations required to do so. But those who recognize the complexity of the phenomena usually agree that it is possible to find a basic explanation, by means of a small number of simple principles, that enables to make almost infinitely varied combinations of some simple elements.

One might believe that an extremely complex discourse can be explained beginning with the structural principles to combine phonemes and words. One might believe to have found a key to biological organization by showing the structure of the double articulation represented by combinations of four letters. Undoubtedly such explanations can go quite far and enable us to understand both unity and diversity. But they do not exhaust all of the problems of explanation. Structural linguistics does not explain the meaning of the discourse. The genetic algorithm explains neither the existence of the phenomena nor this bundle of emerging qualities that we call "life." Molecular biology explained the chemical machinery of life, but not life itself. It believed that life is a mythological notion unworthy of science, and expelled life from biology.

On the contrary, we must question the adequacy of all explanations based on simplification of principles. Complexity is not a surface noise of the real, but is the very principle of the real. The physical foundation of what we call reality is not simple, but is complex. The atom is not simple. The so-called elementary particle is not a simple primary unit. It oscillates between the being and nonbeing, between wave and particle. It may contain nonisolatable components (quarks). At the macrocosmic level, the universe is no longer the ordered sphere that Laplace dreamed of. It is at the same time dispersion and condensation, disintegration and organization. Uncertainty, indeterminism, randomness, and contradictions occur, not as residues to be eliminated by explanation, but as non-eliminatable ingredients of our perception/cognition of the real. All these ingredients, which ruined the principle of reductionistic explanations, now nourish the complex explanations.

We must combine the notions that exclude one another in the framework of the principle of simplification/reduction (Figure 4). The

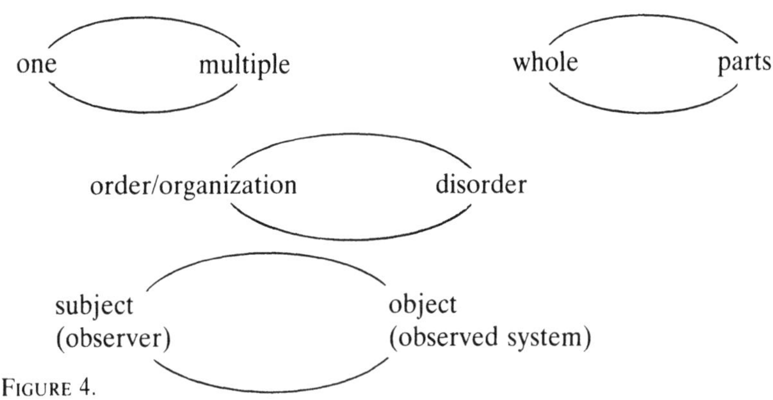

FIGURE 4.

establishment of mutual implications and therefore necessary conjunctions among the notions that are disjoint in classical thinking is shown in Figure 5.

It is complex because it introduces a complex causality, more specifically an eco-auto-causality, where autocausality means recursive causality in which the organizing process elaborates the products, ac-

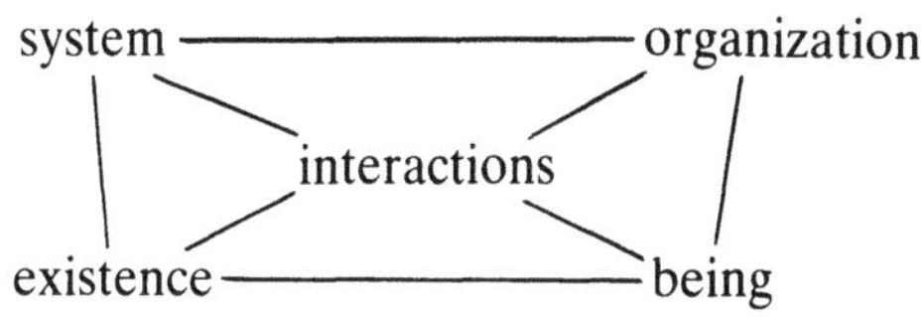

FIGURE 5.

tions, and effects necessary for its creation or regeneration, and where autocausality needs causality from outside.

The Whole is Not a Collection

In opposition to the notion of general or specific theory of systems, I propose a systemic paradigm that would have to be present in all theories regardless of the field of their application.

Holism retrieves only a partial, unidimensional, and simplifying view of the whole. It deforms the concept of totality to a concept, to which other systemic concepts are reduced, whereas it ought to be a concept of confluence. *Holism* arises from a paradigm of simplification, or a reduction of the complexity to a key concept or a key category.

On the other hand, with regard to the new paradigm of system, Pascal had already said: "I consider it impossible to know the parts without the whole, not any more possible than knowing the whole without knowing the specific parts." Out of this formulation by Pascal, we can make a higher level understanding based on the constructive circularity of the explanation of the whole by the parts and the parts by the whole, in which the two explanations become complementary *in the movement associating them* without losing their simultaneous and opposing characteristics (Figure 6).

FIGURE 6.

It is this active loop constitutes the description and the explanation. At the same time, to keep a certain opposition and a certain play between the two processes of explanation, which the simplistic logic would regard as mutually excluding, is not vicious but productive. Furthermore, the search for the explanation in the reverse direction of one of the processes with regard to the other (parts $\rightleftarrows$ whole, whole $\rightleftarrows$ parts) leads to the first introduction of the complexity at the paradigmatic level. This is because, as we shall see, we should not only respect complexity at the level of phenomena but also at the level of the principle, where it should be revealed in the first place.

At the same time, we must see the system not only as a global unity (which is merely to replace the simple elementary unity of reductionism with a macro-unity) but as a *unitas multiplex*, where antagonistic terms are combined. The whole is a macro-unity, but the parts in it are neither merged or confused. They have a double identity: an individual identity that is not reducible to the whole, and a common identity of systemic citizenship. Moreover, the atomic, biological, and social systems show us that a system is not only a composition of unity from diversity, but also that of diversity from unity. Examples are: Pauli's exclusion principle, which creates electronic diversification around a nucleus; biological morphogenesis from an undifferentiated embryo to a complex adult organism; societies that not only give a culture and a common identity to diverse individuals, but also allows, by means of the culture, further development of diversity. Here again, a loop is in operation between two principles of explanation (Figure 7). The unifying thinking alone

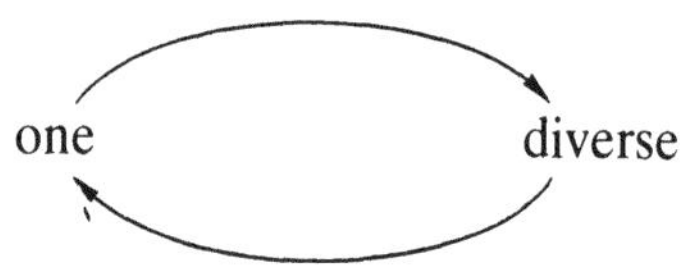

FIGURE 7.

becomes increasingly homogenizing and loses diversity. The differentiating thinking becomes catalogue-like and loses unity. Here again, it is not a matter of "dosage" or "equilibrium" between these two processes of explanation. One has to integrate both in an active loop in which:

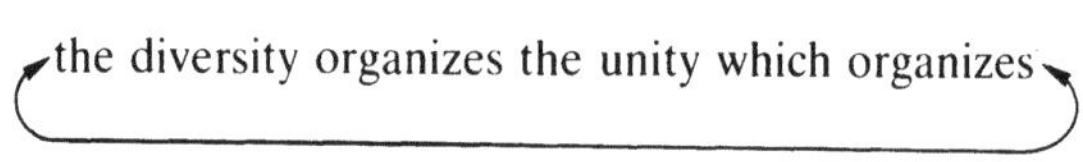

The central problem is not that of maintaining relations of the type whole/parts or one/many, but one must also focus on the complex character of these relations that can be summarized as follows (for details, see Morin, 1977, pp. 105–128):

The whole is more than the sum of the parts. This principle is intuitively recognized at all macroscopic levels, but also *emergences* occur that are of new qualities and properties for the parts.

The whole is less than the sum of the parts because the latter lose some of their qualities or properties under the constraining effects of the organization of the whole.

The whole is more than the whole because the whole acts on the parts that act on the whole. In other words, the whole is more than a global reality. It is an organizational dynamism.

It is in this framework that we must understand the being, the existence, and the life as emerging global qualities. These key notions are not of the primary qualities, root, or essence, but of the realities of emergence. The being and the existence are emergences of the entire process that loops on itself (Morin, 1977, especially pp. 210–216). The life is a bundle of emerging qualities resulting from the process of interaction and organization between the parts and the whole. The emerging bundle acts back on the parts and on the partial and global interactions and processes that produced it. Hence the complex principle of explanation: One must not reduce the phenomenal to the generative, nor the superstructure to the infrastructure. But the explanation must try to understand the process, in which the products or final effects generate their own new beginning. This process is named here "recursive" (Figure 8).

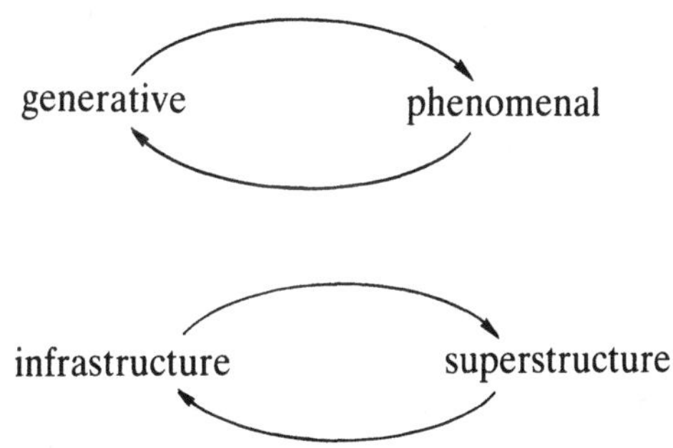

FIGURE 8.

The parts are at the same time more than and less than the parts. The most remarkable emergences in a very complex system such as a human society occur not only at the level of the whole (the society), but also at the level of the individuals. Awareness of the self occurs only in individuals.

In this sense, *the parts may become more than the whole.* "The most profitable control system of the parts should not exclude the bankruptcy of the whole" (Beer, 1960). The "progress" is not necessarily the formation of increasing totalities, but it may be in the freedom and independence of small units. The richness of the universe is not in the expanding totality, but in the reflective, deviating, and pheripheral small units. This fact, noticed by Gunther (1962) and Brown (1962), recaptures a statement by Pascal (1670): "When the universe would crush the humankind, the human being would be nobler than the universe, because he knows that he dies, and the universe knows nothing of the advantage it has over the humankind."

The whole is less than the whole. In everything there are zones of shadow, mutual ignorance, gaps and cracks between the repressed and the expressed, the immersed and the emerging, the generative, and the phenomenal. There are black holes in the core of all biological and especially anthroposocial entities. It is not only the individual who is ignorant and unaware of the social totality, but this social totality is also ignorant and unaware of the dreams, aspirations, thoughts, love, and hatred of the individuals, and billions of cells in each individual are also unaware of them. If we include these concepts of black holes, zones of shadows and gaps as well as the mutual ignorance in the systemic paradigm itself, this latter leads by itself to modern theories of the anthropological unconscious (Freud) and the sociological inconscious (Marx).

The whole is insufficient, which follows from the above.

The whole is uncertain. We shall see later that there is no sure way to isolate or close up a system among systems of systems of systems, to which it is associated and in which it is inserted. It is also uncertain in the sense of polytotalities in the living universe, in which every polytotality can be thought of at the same time as a whole and as a part. As far as Homo sapiens is concerned, what is the system, the society, the species, the individual?

The whole is conflictual. I have attempted to show (Morin, 1977, pp. 118–122, 217–224) that in all systems there are forces antagonistic to their perpetuation. These forces are activated, cancelled, constantly controlled, suppressed (by negative feedback), or used constructively. For example, in astronomy, implosions and explosions constitute spontaneous regulating of the organizing type. The living organizing formation is intelligible only in terms of permanent disorganization, which destroys molecules and cells that in turn are continuously replaced with new ones. At the level of human societies, we must understand *systemically* the concept of Montesquieu, according to which social conflicts have been sources of not only the fall but also the greatness of the Roman empire, as well as Marx's theory that ties the concept of society organized in classes to the concept of antagonism between the classes.

Thus we must base the concept of system on a nontotalitarian and nonhierarchical concept of the whole, on a complex concept of unitas multiplex, open to polytotalities. This preliminary paradigmatic view is of great practical and political importance. The paradigm of holistic simplification leads to a neototalitarian functionalism and adequately merges with all modern forms of totalitarianism. In any case it leads to manipulation of units in the name of the whole. In contrast, the logic of the paradigm of complexity leads not only to a "truer" knowledge, but also to the search for a practice and a policy, both of which are complex. I shall elaborate this point later.

The Psychophysical Character of the Systemic Paradigm

The old paradigm of simplification made it necessary for us to choose between two orders of the systemic reality: (a) a system is a measurable physical category that presents itself to the perception of the observer who must endeavor to make an accurate description of it; or (b) a system is a mental category, or mentally constructed heuristic and/or pragmatic model used for controlling, understanding, or simulating the phenomena.

The new complex conceptualization of the system cannot be accommodated in either of the alternatives. The system is a concept with double entry:

$$\text{Physis} \rightleftharpoons \text{psyche}$$

The concept has physical feet and a psychic head. It is:

physical	psychic
by formation and by existence (interaction, combination of ecological circumstances, energetic and thermodynamic conditions and operations). Even a system of thinking has a physical component (biochemicophysical processes related to cerebral activities).	by distinction and isolation, by the choice of successively nesting concepts (subsystem, system, suprasytem, ecosystem).

from which we obtain:
a principle of the art (of diagnostics);
a principle of critical reflection
(on the relativity of the notions of the boundaries of systems);
a principle of uncertainty.

Hence the indivisibility of the psychic/physical character of the system, and the indivisibility of the relation subject/object or observer/observed, and consequently the necessity to include the observer in the observation instead of excluding him from it.

It is necessary to elaborate a metasystem of comprehension in which the system of observation/perception/concept-formation has to be observed, perceived, and conceptualized in the observed system which is observing itself. Therefore we have a chain of consequences that leads us to complexify our mode of perceiving and conceptualizing the world of phenomena. We must proceed to a paradigmatic and epistemological reform that is more important than what we saw until now, because the articulation between the knowledge of organization and the organization of knowledge calls for a reorganization of knowledge by introducing a second-degree reflectivity, i.e., a knowledge of the knowledge.

At the same time, the dichotomy between physical sciences and mental sciences, between the sciences of nature and the science of the culture, between the biophysical sciences and the anthroposocial sciences seems to us to be a premature mutilation and an obstacle to all serious knowledge. If the desire to articulate these disjoint sciences seems grotesque, then the acceptance of this disjunction becomes even more grotesque.

If we are still incapable of making the new articulation needed, we must at least put the following side-by-side:

the observer	the observed system
the subject	the object
the culture (which produces a physical science)	the physis (which produces biological organization that produces anthroposocial organization, hence culture)

The operation of distinguishing, which is basic to all cognitive acts, becomes complex. It appears to be a result of a transaction between the observer and the observed world, during which one of the partners can very well fool the other. The way of making cognitive distinction is embedded in a culture which provides paradigms permitting and requiring the distinction. It has therefore an ideological characteristic among other characteristics. Even though one should not reduce science to ideology (in other words to see science merely as an ideological product of the society), one must be aware that an ideological component enters any scientific knowledge. We cannot afford to skip examining the ideological aspect of the scientific knowledge including one's own knowledge. This applies also to thoese who believe that they have the true science and denounce the ideology of others.

The Systemized Theories

The system is a generic concept better than a general concept. It is generic in a new mode of thinking useful in a general way. On the other hand a general theory of systems is not needed if one looks for general applicability. The systemic organizational dimension ought to be present in all theories on physical, biological, anthroposociological, and conceptual universe. These theories, if they were branches of a general theory of systems, would reduce the diverse phenomena captured by human senses to one of the systemic dimensions without making connections among many dimensions. But each of the phenomena has its physics, chemistry, thermodynamics, nature, organization, being, and existence. We must therefore differentiate between theories relating to types of phenomena.

We must add that the general systems theory as applied to biological and social systems, but based only on the notion of open system, is completely insufficient. Therefore it seems necessary to return to the physical, biological, and anthroposociological theories, to go deeper in their systemic-organizational dimension, and to articulate them (a) in the key concepts of organization, and (b) in a way of thinking capable of operating the loops among terms that are at the same time complementary, concurrent, and antagonistic.

Otherwise, one falls back into the vices of reduction, homogenization, and abstraction, which the theory of systems claims to remedy.

Conclusions

1. The system is not the masterword for the totality. It is a root word for complexity.
2. One must elevate the concept of system from the theoretical level to the paradigmatic level. The same can be said of the concept of cybernetics of machines.
3. It is not a matter of making a general theory including the atom, the molecule, the star, the cell, the organization, the artifact, and the society. The problem is to reconsider them all in a richer way in the light of the systemic/organizational complexity, including our own reality.
4. Under the domination of the paradigm of simplification/disjunction, the being, the existence, and the life dissolve into systemic abstraction which perpetuates all the abstractions obscuring the richness of the real and resulting in unrestrained manipulation. On the contrary, under the effect of the development of the complex concept of system/organization, the being, the existence, and the life suddenly emerge.
5. As long as the systemic idea remains theoretical, it does not change the paradigm of disjunction/simplification which it believes to have overcome by overcoming the reductionistic atomization. However, its "holism" becomes reductionistic by reducing everything to the

whole. It is only at the paradigmatic level where its complexiety truly florishes that the systemic can open itself to a new complex organization of thought and action.

6. A new rationality shows a glimpse of itself. The old rationality sought only to harvest order in nature. But it fished fishbones, not fish. The new rationality enables one to perceive fish and ocean by allowing to conceptualize organization and existence; in other words, it enables one to perceive that which cannot be fished.
7. The old theory organized by orders from top down. But one must begin with organization, in other words with the play of interactions between the involved parts and the whole. In this sense, "to organize " must replace "to order." The more complex the organization, the more it contains disorder called "freedom."
8. Organization is not institution. It is a regenerative and generative activity always present at all levels, based on computation, elaboration of strategies, communication, and dialogue.
9. The systemic paradigm requires us to master, not the nature, but our own art of mastering. This opens to us forms of action containing the awareness and control of the self.
10. Such a principle opens a way to a responsible, liberal, radically different, and community-oriented practice. Each of these terms is transformed by its interaction with the others. This practice leads to a rediscovery of the problem of wisdom and the necessity to build our wisdom. The search for this wisdom is in this sense a search for a way to overcome the fissure that developed in the Western world between the universe of meditation and that of social practice.

References

Beer, Stafford. (1960). Below the twilight arch. In *General Systems Yearbook*.
Brown, Spencer. (1972). *The Laws of Form*. New York: Bantam Books.
Günther, Gottard. (1962). Cybernetical ontology and transformational operation. In Yovits, Marshall C. and Cameron, Scott (Eds), *Self-organizing systems*, New York: Pergamon.
Morin, Edgar. (1977). *La Méthode*. Paris: Seuil.
Pascal, Blaise. (1670). *Pensées*. (New edition 1976, Paris: Mercure de France).

Author Index

Subject Index

Italic page numbers indicate definitions of terms

MIX
Papier aus verantwortungsvollen Quellen
Paper from responsible sources
FSC® C105338

If you have any concerns about our products,
you can contact us on
ProductSafety@springernature.com

In case Publisher is established outside the EU,
the EU authorized representative is:
Springer Nature Customer Service Center GmbH
Europaplatz 3, 69115 Heidelberg, Germany

Printed by Libri Plureos GmbH
in Hamburg, Germany